psychotherapist Tirzah Firestone lets us listen in to the powerful stories of people who have suffered trauma in their lives. She offers us the wisdom of a compassionate therapist whose understanding is broad and deep. But she also offers us the spiritual perspective of a rabbi who has found her way to the deeper currents of Jewish understanding. Running through WOUNDS INTO WISDOM, and binding it, is an autobiographical account of her own family's trauma. That account is powerful in itself, but it is also empowering—we can feel how the author has herself lived through trauma, and has even found her way to become a great healer and teacher. The book is addressed primarily to the Jewish experience of trauma in the twentieth century. But I believe it would be of profound help to anyone seeking to navigate the path to healing from trauma—which I believe, in some ways, is all of us."—**Rodger Kamenetz, author of *The Jew in the Lotus* and *The History of Last Night's Dream***

"WOUNDS INTO WISDOM is a tour de force! Rabbi Firestone has woven together threads of truth about trauma that include her own family's life-experience of trauma inherited from the Holocaust, the new science of the inherited effects of trauma on genetic material and on the brain, studies of the social impact of traumatic events on large groups of people, and the mystical traditions of Kabbalah about the wounded human soul. She has woven these threads into a shimmering shawl of healing."—**Rabbi Arthur Waskow, director of The Shalom Center and author of *Godwrestling—Round 2* and *Torah of the Earth: Exploring 4,000 Years of Ecology in Jewish Thought***

"With tender compassion and luminous insight, Rabbi Tirzah unwraps the hidden layers of stories, wounds, and wisdom that characterize the global Jewish community. She deftly lifts the complex history of modern Judaism to the light, offering an opportunity for particular reconciliation and universal healing."—**Mirabai Starr, author of *God of Love: A Guide to the Heart of Judaism, Christianity and Islam* and *Caravan of No Despair: A Memoir of Loss and Transformation***

Advance praise for

Wounds into Wisdom:

"Suffering trauma is tragedy enough, but burying tragedy only creates a magnet for more suffering. Tirzah Firestone's WOUNDS INTO WISDOM *is for anyone who has suffered trauma, either directly or in a family whose generational trauma is buried.* It helps readers uncover suffering and use it to help others—the final stage of healing. We may not be able to control what happens to us, but we can create what happens *next."*—**Gloria Steinem**

"An explosion of suffering, death and trauma has overtaken humanity during the past century and shows no signs of abating. Rabbi Tirzah Firestone speaks on every page of this deeply moving book with her heart and mind and from the deepest wellsprings of Jewish tradition to find sources of solace to transform wounds into wisdom. Her book spills over with empathy and compassion, forging a uniquely spiritual voice that heals and lifts our souls." —**Susannah Heschel, Eli Black Professor of Jewish Studies, Dartmouth College and editor of *Abraham Joshua Heschel: Essential Writings***

"If we are ever to transform conflict and bring peace to this wounded world, we will need to understand and address collective and intergenerational trauma. In this illuminating and inspiring book, Rabbi Tirzah Firestone interweaves deeply touching personal stories including her own with keen psychological insights to guide us on a journey of awakening and healing our traumas. Highly recommended!"—**William Ury, co-author of the bestsellers *Getting to Yes* and author of *Getting to Yes with Yourself***

"This book is both a gift of wisdom and an opening of the heart. Representing years and years of feeling research, rabbi and

"A very important book. Rabbi Tirzah is a wounded healer. She uses the tale of her own trauma in a Holocaust survivor family as a stepping stone toward understanding survivor stories told by a wide variety of Jews, including many Israelis. But she then broadens the lens, showing how these very particularistic tales of personal struggle and healing may help people of many cultures to deal with legacies of exile and loss. A narrative of deep empathy and much wisdom."—**Professor Art Green, Founding Dean of Hebrew College, Boston, and author of *Judaism's Ten Best Ideas* and *Radical Judaism***

"WOUNDS INTO WISDOM is a book to share and spread. Rabbi Tirzah Firestone's compassionate wisdom shines through every page as she leads her readers on a journey toward freedom and healing from communal trauma. Transformation no longer seems like a wishful aspiration, it is a birthright we all have the power to claim."—**Naomi Levy, author of *Einstein and the Rabbi***

"Brilliant, beautiful, and compels one to positive action. The people interviewed are so real and lovable.... [Firestone's] writing opens one's heart to healing and hope. This is a book I will read again for inspiration and specific principles to live a joyful, liberated life."—**Dr. Anita L. Sanchez, author of *The Four Sacred Gifts: Indigenous Wisdom for Modern Times***

"Drawing on remarkable, true stories and tantalizing psychological and scientific theories that trace trauma in previous generations to subsequent ones, Rabbi Tirzah Firestone makes a strong case that the experiences of past generations live on in us. She provides a convincing case in remarkably clear language. WOUNDS INTO WISDOM is a powerful game-changer in how we will come to view trauma."—**Howard Schwartz, editor of *Tree of Souls: The Mythology of Judaism***

"WOUNDS INTO WISDOM is a timely and moving book that speaks to this particular historical moment, when current events are triggering deeply buried trauma and traumatizing new populations. Firestone makes a clear and urgent case for the importance of this work and its application to different contexts, and grounding it in her own family's story makes the book come alive."—**Judith Rosenbaum, Ph.D., Executive Director of the Jewish Women's Archive**

"Tirzah Firestone's WOUNDS INTO WISDOM offers hope to those whose lives have been shattered by trauma. The question at the heart of this book is this: Can you emerge from tragedy wiser and more free? Her answer eloquently stated and illustrated by powerful stories and profound insight, is yes you can. If tragedy haunts your life or the lives of those you love—read this book; it has the potential to change everything."—**Rabbi Rami Shapiro, author of *Minyan* and annotation of sacred teachings in *Perennial Wisdom for the Spiritually Independent***

"We all fear trauma and take pains to avoid or bury it. As a result, trauma can lodge in the body or the unconscious, and, as Tirzah Firestone writes in this compelling book, can be passed unknowingly from generation to generation, 'like a train depositing its load, car after car, into our newborn skin.' The power of this book is in the stories she relates of people who've suffered extreme pain, faced it head-on, and found a path to healing. The stories soften our hearts, inspire gratitude and compassion for our fellow humans, and give us the tools to make sure the train of trauma goes no further."—**Sara Davidson, *New York Times* bestselling author of *The December Project, Loose Change,* and *Joan: Forty Years of Life, Loss, and Friendship with Joan Didion***

"Tirzah Firestone is a compelling and genuinely fresh voice, revealing over and over again 'resonant truths that hold meaning for today.' I am moved by this book. And even when I disagree with her, Firestone makes me think in a broader way, as she will you."—**Rabbi Joseph Telushkin, author of *Jewish Literacy* and *Jewish Wisdom***

Wounds into Wisdom

Healing Intergenerational Jewish Trauma

Rabbi Tirzah Firestone, Ph.D.

ADAM KADMON BOOKS /
MONKFISH BOOK PUBLISHING COMPANY
RHINEBECK, NEW YORK

Hardcover ISBN 978-1-948626-02-6
eBook ISBN 978-1-948626-03-3

Library of Congress Cataloging-in-Publication Data

Names: Firestone, Tirzah, author.
Title: Wounds into wisdom : healing intergenerational Jewish trauma / Rabbi
    Tirzah Firestone, Ph.D.
Description: Rhinebeck, New York : Monkfish Book Publishing, [2019].
Identifiers: LCCN 2018052778 (print) | LCCN 2018055017 (ebook) | ISBN
    9781948626033 (ebook) | ISBN 9781948626026 (hardcover : alk. paper)
Subjects: LCSH: Holocaust, Jewish (1939-1945)--Psychological aspects. |
    Psychic trauma--Transmission. | Psychic trauma--Social aspects. |
    Holocaust survivors--Psychology. | Children of Holocaust
    survivors--Psychology.
Classification: LCC D804.3 (ebook) | LCC D804.3 .F56723 2019 (print) | DDC
    362.87089/924--dc23
LC record available at https://lccn.loc.gov/2018052778

Cover design by Nita Ybarra
Book design by Colin Rolfe

Adam Kadmon Books, a joint imprint of Monkfish Book Publishing Company
and Albion-Andalus

Monkfish Book Publishing Company
22 East Market Street, Suite 304
Rhinebeck, New York 12572
(845) 876-4861

monkfishpublishing.com
albionandalus.com

In memory of my brother Daniel and my sister Shulamith

TABLE OF CONTENTS

PART I

PART II

PART I

INTRODUCTION

Shedding New Light on a Dark History

IN MY TWENTY-FIFTH YEAR, I dreamed of a slender Hungarian woman dressed in a fur coat. Beneath her lavish attire, I saw that she was, in fact, a naked skeleton, peering at me with both irony and affection. The woman could see that I was young and raw, paralyzed by an unnamed guilt, barely able to buy myself a teapot or a secondhand sweater without being assailed by self-doubt.

Dahlink, she called to me, her thick accent comforting and somehow familiar: *Don't be a fool! Don't you think we would be enjoying our beautiful things if we could?* Her jaw clacked with boney laughter.

Suddenly the lights went on and the room filled with richly clad Hungarian ladies, skeletons all, enjoying a tea party. It was clear that they were all dead, yet they were also radiant and full of life. Turning toward me, their voices rose in unison: *Do you think it helps us that you suffer? Live the life we could not live!*

I sat up in bed and wept. Their words had penetrated me, touching the core of my malaise, an outsized case of survivor's guilt I did not know I had. *Live the life we could not live!* These words became a turning point, a mantra, a north star. I took them with me as I found my footing in the world, followed the call to become a psychotherapist, and ultimately, rejoined the religion that I had fled.

But it was not until fifteen years later that I learned the truth of my dream. I learned that my German grandmother's entire family came from Austro-Hungary; almost all had been murdered in Nazi Europe. Their elegant bearing had not helped them one wit to escape Hitler's roundups; their assimilation into high society meant nothing in the end. Stripped of all their beautiful things, they died like paupers in the death camps.

Like many post-Holocaust families, my parents did not speak directly of these matters. The heavy legacy of loss remained muted. Yet for my five siblings and me, it was like finding ourselves in deep waters without life vests or instruction. We responded as best we could, each of us fighting the undertow of history, swimming or sinking, not knowing how to help one another, divided by the trauma we had inherited, but never knowing why.

Scholars of intergenerational trauma tell us that the silence shrouding a family's untold stories paradoxically becomes the strongest form of transmission.[1] This was the case in my own family, and in myriad families with whom I have worked as rabbi and psychotherapist.

Yet, there is an inner compulsion to know. "One has to know one's buried truth in order to be able to live one's life," writes the late Professor Dori Laub, himself a survivor.[2] Many of us struggle to bring to consciousness the hidden legacies that our families bequeath to us. For some, it takes years to piece together the unspoken wounds that have shaped our lives. The residue of our ancestors' unresolved injury does not simply disappear. In fact, it often weighs most heavily on the introspective, sensitive members of the next generations.

~~~~~~~~~~~~~~~~

Beginning with the stories of my own family and the post-Holocaust community that shaped my young life, this book combines insights from recent scientific research with the voices of Jewish survivors and their descendants from around the world. Among others, we will hear from Avi, who was sent out into the streets of Krakow as a four-year-old and lived to become an Israeli military hero; Esti, whose entire family was haunted by a tragic secret left behind in Iran; Rami, who lost his daughter in a suicide bombing and joined forces with a bereaved Palestinian to grieve and speak out; and from many others, from college students to octogenarians.

The search that became this book began inside a progressive American Jewish community, where for two decades I led a flourishing congregation and came into contact with people at every stage of living and dying. There I watched, studied, and counseled Jewish families as they resurrected life in the second, third, and now, fourth generations after the Holocaust. Brilliance, creativity, reactivity, agitation, and often a sense of profound urgency and unsafety in the world characterized many of the people with whom I met.

Before becoming a rabbi, I had trained in counseling. Feeling compelled to learn more, I began doctoral studies in psychology. Eventually, my research brought me to Jewish Israel, where I interviewed trauma survivors of racial persecution and their descendants; those who had lost children to terror attacks and military incidents; and those who suffered the kind of trauma that is now being termed "moral injury"[3] in the context of war and occupation.

Although Israeli life overflows with color and the cultural richness born of the intermingling of Jewish populations from around the world, most Jewish Israelis harbor some trauma resulting from past racial or religious discrimination. This history is complicated by current wars and an ongoing existential threat created by Israel's precarious location and relationships with its neighbors.

As I saw again and again, the consequences of large-scale ethnic trauma correspond to those of individual post-traumatic stress disorder (PTSD). Symptoms such as emotional numbing, hyperreactivity, shame, isolation, and the inadvertent compulsion to reenact traumatic injuries appear similarly in the aftermath of both individual and collective trauma.

Recent advances in neuroscience and psychology also gave me a new understanding of the intergenerational effects of trauma. For example, as I'll discuss in Chapter Two, the field of epigenetics offers growing evidence that traumatic events can create a kind of "biological memory" that emerges under stress. One landmark study carried out in Jerusalem found that the descendants of parents, grandparents, and even great-grandparents who endured persecution, war, and other extreme stresses were prone to depression, anxiety, and other stress responses remarkably similar to those of their ancestors.[4]

──────────

For Jews today, who still live in the shadow of war, racial persecution, and terror attacks, the traits of resilience, resourcefulness, loyalty to tribe, and fierce determination—cultivated over generations of adversity—are unmistakable. But the harmful byproducts of Jewish historical trauma must also be acknowledged. Left unexamined, they may jeopardize the ethical vision of a proud culture that has survived for thousands of years.

Although my research began with a study of damage, I became increasingly focused on healing. I asked: *Is it possible to transform the effects of historical trauma? To come through life's heavy blows with more wisdom and a sense of inner freedom?*

The answer is yes. The individuals whose journeys I recount here did the deep work, each in their own way, of facing their injuries and transforming them. We follow them across the world, into the bomb shelters of Sderot, on boats to Shanghai, in the New York subway, and on the battlefront of Hebron. All of these people remind us of our own human capacity to rise up after devastation with profound wisdom and inner freedom.

I owe them endless thanks for sharing their lives with me. In so many cases, they were eager for their stories to be heard, with the hope that the telling of their lives might deepen an understanding of Jewish historical trauma and alleviate suffering for others. In some cases, at their request, I have changed names to protect their privacy. However, all words in quotation marks are the words that they spoke.

The seven principles in Part II emerged directly from their testimonies. They teach us that we can survive extreme trauma and be changed in radically positive ways. At the broadest level, they are seven directives for staying morally awake in a world rife with terror.

The study of Jewish trauma has awakened me to the vastness of the problem of collective trauma. All over the world, cultures and groups are being dislocated by war, poverty, and climatic changes, and fresh wounds are being incurred daily—to refugees, religious groups, indigenous tribes, and entire ethnicities. The more we understand the ways in which trauma works, and the deeper our compassion for the plight of those who suffer—including our ancestors and our own selves—the more we have to offer our world.

I have learned that we can recognize, choose, and redefine our own destinies, even in the aftermath of ruinous events. Humans are created with the capacity to heal from wreckage, transform fear into compassion, and turn tragedy into strength. The power to heal lives within each of us.

CHAPTER ONE

The Price of Silence

THE FATE OF MY MOTHER'S family remained unmentioned until I was forty. That year I received a strange phone call. On the other end of the phone was a raspy male voice speaking in a thick hybrid accent. Thinking it a prank, I prepared to hang up, but the voice on the other end protested loudly.

"Don't hang up! I am your cousin from Australia, and I am very sad you don't know nothing about your family. You don't know you even have a cousin like me, do you?"

"*What?* Who is this?"

"I am Ziggy, your mother's cousin."

Over the next half hour, through Ziggy's German-turned-Aussie accent, I gathered his story. He and his family had been rounded up in 1942 from Topolcany, a tiny town in present-day Slovakia. Managing to escape the Nazi labor camp to which he'd been sent, Ziggy lived in a nearby forest, surviving with meager help from an underground resistance group. At war's end, not yet twenty years old, he had found himself in a displaced person's camp, where he soon learned that his parents and brother, uncles, aunts, and cousins had all died. Where should he go?

From the *Israelische Kultusgemeinde*, the Jewish Cultural Center based in Prague, Ziggy learned that one family of cousins had succeeded in escaping Europe in time. It was my mother, her four siblings, and parents. Joyfully, Ziggy sent a letter to his aunt, my grandmother, in Canada.

"But then how did you end up in Australia? Didn't she send for you?"

"Well, your grandmother was trying to get me a permit to come to the States as a student in a Baltimore Yeshiva," Ziggy told me. "She wanted me to adopt a Jewish life. But I had seen too many horrors. I wasn't keen on being a *yeshiva bocher*[1] after what I had gone through. I decided to go in the opposite direction. That's how I came here to Australia. No one here to tell me how I should live."

I took a liking to Ziggy. I too had tried to flee the freighted, overbearing nature of our family's legacy. Both of us had come back around in time, with Ziggy rejoining the Jewish community in Sydney and then emigrating to Israel; and I, after abandoning our birth religion and intermarrying, returning to embrace and study Judaism, ultimately becoming a rabbi.

It was from Ziggy that I learned the dark truth about my maternal ancestors. Few had made it out. My mother and her immediate family were the lucky ones. She had buried the others with her grief, submerging memories of her lost relatives beyond conscious reach.

We now understand that unprocessed trauma does not simply disappear. But how could my mother have known this? In fact, it was not until after the Vietnam War, in 1980, that post-traumatic stress disorder was officially recognized, acquiring a name and an official diagnosis.[2]

Much later in life, when dementia set in and her defenses had softened, Mom suffered from unpredictable paroxysms of shock and terror. Sudden news flashes seemed to break through into her consciousness out of the blue, as if announcing the death of beloved relatives for the first time. Sobbing over the unexpected news of her losses, she would ask again and again: *Why didn't anyone tell me?*

Her first cousin Ziggy took a different approach. Having lost both parents, his brother, and his cousins in the gas chambers, Ziggy chose to spend his adult life facing into his losses. He became a genealogist, researching and collecting information on the whereabouts of every close and distant relative, how and where they died, and who had made it out alive. His first call to me from Australia had been part of that project. By the end of his life in 2012, Ziggy had published his research in book form, an extensive family tree honoring every member of his family.

Ziggy and my mother became my models for the choices we face in dealing with our traumatic memories. My mother had buried the horrors of the war, while Ziggy had chosen to dive into its particulars. Mom did not know and had no one to tell her that there is ultimately no running from profound pain. She did what many do: turning away from tragedy and getting on with life. Although this choice can reflect toughness and dignity, the price we pay is often a progressive narrowing and shutting down.

The path Ziggy took is more sustainable. He not only acknowledged his trauma, he gave it a context and purpose. By taking on a task informed by his life's catastrophe, he succeeded in transforming his grief.

As I learned from Ziggy and from my later research, the capacity to put our pain into context is key, allowing us to acknowledge its power, yet give it boundaries. Traumatic memory torments us and will own us if we do not contain it. But when we face and acknowledge it, it may then be possible to convert it to something positive.

──────── *My Father's Hidden Pictures* ────────

My father, Sol, was a Jew from Brooklyn who was serving in the U.S. Army Air Corps when he met my mother in Detroit in 1942. Beautiful and wide-eyed at age twenty-three, Kate had just made her way to the United States from England, where the *Kindertransport* had deposited her. She had been saved by this noble rescue effort, which brought 10,000 Jewish children from throughout continental Europe to safety in Great Britain just before the outbreak of World War II.

Sol and Kate met at a Young Israel synagogue mixer. They were an unlikely match. Kate (whose Yiddish name was Gittel) descended from a lineage of strictly Orthodox rabbis and cantors from Austro-Hungary. Sol, on the other hand, was raised in an assimilated Jewish American household. What he lacked in Jewish training, he made up for in enthusiasm. He had recently become an ardent born-again Orthodox Jew.

Dad cut a strapping figure in his army uniform. He had a full head of hair then, and wore his signature mustache.

Before the war, Dad had presciently schooled himself in Japanese and German, dabbling in business deals and picking up sporadic work as a translator. He was stationed in Salt Lake City, where his first son, Danny, was born. This was an auspicious start to their marriage.

My mother was pregnant again when Dad was deployed to Japan for what was almost sure to be a fatal mission. Then, at the last minute, a Jewish staff sergeant changed his papers and rerouted him to Germany. Dad shipped out in January, 1945, just days after Kate delivered their second child, a girl they named Shulamith.

While Dad was overseas, Mom and her two babies moved in with her German-speaking parents in Ottawa. When Dad returned to his young family after the war, he was a changed man. And like many returning soldiers, he never discussed his war experiences, maintaining his silence until he died in Israel in 1981.

It was only upon reading his obituary that I learned what Dad had experienced in Germany. Serving on a prestigious but deadly bomb disposal squadron, his assignments took him to the most devastated parts of the country. And then in April, 1945, just days after its liberation, he entered what remained of the Bergen-Belsen concentration camp where British troops were tending survivors and clearing over an acre of ground covered with corpses and those dying of disease, starvation, and lack of medical attention.

Now, after his death, his children found photographs hidden away in his files: shocking images that he had taken inside the death camp: vermin-infested barracks; stacked, decaying corpses; abandoned Nazi warplanes.

These horrifying pictures had been concealed from us and from conscious conversation for thirty-six years. But the impact of his experience could not be hidden. The emotional charge behind Dad's buried images and untold stories had come through loud and clear.

─────────── *Passing Down Trauma* ───────────

I can still see those vile images my father had recorded of the death camp as a young man. The sepia photographs of ravaged human corpses and the squalid conditions of their enslavement horrified me. Yet they were also strangely familiar. Long before I had ever laid my physical eyes on them, I had somehow picked up on the barbarity of these photographs from the shared ethers of my family's post-Holocaust world.

Since then I have learned that children's psychic borders are highly permeable. From our earliest moments when we have yet to distinguish ourselves as separate entities, we receive all manner of impressions from the adults around us, which become part of our internal reality. Like feelings that echo between people, creating a syntonic resonance, studies show that mental images too, can be transferred, especially to youngsters.[3]

Every war and catastrophic event carries its own images that imprint themselves upon the collective mind: naked children fleeing a napalm attack in Vietnam, the Twin Towers billowing with smoke, a Syrian child washed up on the shores of a foreign land. These images arouse a multitude of feelings and associations. One might say that such strong mental representations are "viscerally inscribed" within us.

In the aftermath of traumatic events, it is extremely common for strong mental images to be harbored in our minds, playing and replaying themselves. I propose that these unintegrated memory fragments can be transmitted, or "deposited" within young, porous minds by their parents and caregivers. This is largely an unconscious process. While in most cases the experiences and memories that created these mental pictures are not registered, the trauma images and feeling tone that carries them are often transmitted and received. As we have seen, such transmissions occur with more force when silence and heightened stress accompany them.

In this, I am following the work of Dr. Vamik Volkan, internationally acclaimed psychoanalyst in the field of collective trauma, who has spent his professional life studying the effects of war, terror, and displacement on the psychology of populations around the world. Volkan calls the transmission of trauma from one generation to the next, *image deposits*. He maintains that traumatized adults can unconsciously deposit their internalized images into the developing self of the child, who then becomes a *reservoir* for the adult's trauma images, which can shape the child's life.[4]

Volkan's experiences in war-ravaged areas taught him that "even persons who have no actual war experiences are influenced to one degree or another by mental images of wars or warlike conditions, due to identifications, transgenerational transmissions, and psychological links to their parents' or ancestors' history."[5]

But images are only one means of transmitting overwhelming experiences.[6] Trauma is embedded in the nervous system through all of our senses. For my childhood friend Ilana, whose family had escaped Hungary, the transmission of trauma was made by means of sound. Whenever an airplane thundered overhead, Ilana would shudder and take cover under the nearest desk or table, imagining it was a bomber.

For Amichai, whose father and uncle had escaped Buchenwald (though his grandparents and many others perished there), World War II trauma was overwhelmingly visual. Amichai's childhood home was filled with family photos, and from a young age he watched war newsreels and Holocaust documentaries on Israeli television. He told me about the behaviors he adopted as a child to help him cope.

"When I go to a movie I always sit at the far end of a row. I need to be able to exit, just in case *they* show up. You know, the Nazis," Amichai added. "And I can't do lines. Every line reminds me of *the* lines. As a kid, I'd be at some wedding at a hotel and see a buffet. I'd go to the head of the line and say, 'Hey I'm from a family of survivors, I don't do lines.' People would say: 'What?' And I'd say, 'I know it doesn't sound right, but believe me, I don't do lines.'"

───────── *Making Meaning of Barbarity* ─────────

The legacy of my father's trauma in Bergen-Belsen—what he saw there and the feelings that ensued over the cruel dehumanization of his people—indirectly became part of our daily fare. In our home, life hovered at boiling point. Family time was filled with fraught lectures on the miracle of Jewish survival, loyalty to Judaism, and the unforgivable crime of interfaith marriage. The latter was tantamount to giving Hitler a *posthumous victory*, according to our father.[7]

The persecution of Jews by the *goyim* (non-Jews) from time immemorial was also a central theme that found its way into most of our dinner conversations. It went without saying that we Jews had survived because we were God's chosen people.

Another theme was the extraordinary number of Jewish Nobel laureates, virtuoso musicians, scientists, businessmen, and even athletes. For Sol, every exceptional person was potentially a Jew, from Alexander the Great to Christopher Columbus (whom Dad was certain was a *converso,* a hidden Jew fleeing the Spanish Inquisition). Henry Kissinger, Sandy Koufax, and even the Barbie and Ken dolls were all famous Jews in his Judeo-centric worldview.

Once I had seen Dad's war photos when I was an adult, I understood the high voltage he carried inside of himself all those years, and the high stakes with which he lived his life. The images he brought back with him from the war were emblazoned in his mind, and I imagine that his entire world had subtly organized itself around them.

For Sol and so many veterans of war who have seen the unseeable and ingested the undigestible, traumatic images are more than just vile and inconceivable. They threaten the very foundation of life. My father struggled to fit the things he had witnessed within the proximate range of a moral universe. He had to supply meaning to the sheer barbarity that had shifted his axis. One way he did this was to understand that Jews were special and distinct from all other people. The world had proved their specialness by hating us. Jews had proved it by surviving.

As we will explore in coming chapters, when confronted with experiences that overwhelm our senses, such as violent acts of war or the suffering and death of innocent people, humans react in a variety of ways. One common coping strategy, or adaptation, is to build walls that seal off the overwhelming feelings of helplessness that accompany the event; to cover over the sensory memories that embed themselves in our nervous systems with a compensatory bravado. When I imagine the feelings of utter vulnerability that Dad must have experienced in the war, which he later overrode with bluster, rage, and incontrovertible opinions, I could more easily forgive his heavy-handed parenting.

Post-War Echoes

It isn't only families who suffer in the aftermath of war, but entire communities. Growing up in the shadow of massive trauma is something like walking onto the site of a fatal train wreck just after it has been cleared of debris. The crush of life still screeches; shock waves still reverberate. And there is a smell of things not being right, even when, on the surface, perfume and smiles dominate.

This was the air that my community breathed in the aftermath of the Holocaust. For us kids, there was an understanding that terrible things had happened. But who dared to ask?

I knew this was the case for Gila, my pale and sensitive friend from Hebrew day school. Her mother, a stocky Slavic woman, had survived the war but had recently died of breast cancer. Her father, an elderly rabbi with a long white beard and ominous eyes, rarely spoke, and when he did, it was in Yiddish or thickly accented English. When we played games outside, Gila refused to run. Her father had warned her not to wear out the soles of her shoes.

Gila had four siblings, and word was that this was the rabbi's second family. His first wife and children had all died in the gas chambers. He had somehow made it out of the camps. Yet there was no sense of a miracle about him.

Other parents spoke in thick accents, too. (I was told that my own mother had a German accent, though I could not hear it.) Several had numbers tattooed on their arms. One of my earliest memories is of gathering around a man in synagogue as he rolled up his sleeve to show us kids his ink markings.

This was all part of life in our Midwestern Jewish neighborhood: the hushed stories; the muted weeping on the women's side of the synagogue; the heavy pall that descended on holidays at *Yizkor*, memorial time, when the air grew thick and an occasional uncontrollable burst of emotion broke loose. A different kind of gravity—more like defiant pride—entered the room at the mention of the State of Israel. It was universally understood that Israel was our miracle and hope, a phoenix risen from the ashes of the Nazis' genocide, sacrosanct in every regard.

During the Six Day War, daily prayer assemblies were held in the auditorium of my Hebrew day school. The memory of these gatherings moves me to this day: Two hundred children from kindergarten through ninth grade prayed their hearts out, weeping for the survival of the state. We were simply and desperately praying for our lives. Later, one of our religious teachers, Rabbi Eichler, himself a survivor, quivered as he told us that it was due to the prayers of Jewish children around the world that the miracle of victory had occurred.

Now I have words for such powerful waves of emotion. I understand how the post-war years were for many of its victims a slow and agonizing process, something like the extreme pain of a frozen limb thawing out and coming back to life. Coming to terms with the knowledge of atrocities committed upon loved ones can elicit wild swings of emotion from shame and demoralization to rage and utter futility.

But as a child in an insulated Jewish neighborhood, there was no other reality—apart from the trim, starchy families I saw on television—with which to compare our lives. Joy certainly did not play a central role. Rather, waves of shock alongside indignation, superiority, fear, and rage—these were all familiar yet unnamed feelings that figured daily in those young years.

As in most post-war Jewish communities, this was also a time of great activity. My parents and their friends were single-minded in their responsibilities of raising their families and putting together funds to build synagogues, day schools, and religious programs. Israel bonds were a staple, as important as food. So was sending money to found Israeli hospitals, orphanages, and free-loan societies. A trip to the Holy Land in those years was considered a hallowed event.

These efforts were made proudly and with fervor. Yet at the same time, as if hidden behind the cupboard doors, another life was festering. In that hushed world the imagination was full of whisperings: stories about children who had been left behind in the middle of the night with a strange family; living hidden in the woods like animals with other young people; silencing a baby's cries with chloroform to smuggle it across borders; and hiding in attics, barns, and below the floorboards for years.

Such stories were never discussed, say, at the dinner table. I had no idea, for example, what my own mother and her siblings had felt leaving behind all their cousins and the entire world of their childhood. I only knew that they had gotten out just in time.

———————————— *Distant Travels* ————————————

I left home at seventeen. Without consciously realizing it, I began studying strangers, intrigued by the behaviors of individuals and families whom I met. Families who enjoyed sporting events or craft projects together were a curiosity. Such diversions were seen as frivolous in my parents' home, where reading and Jewish studies were the acceptable pastimes. Out in the world, people laughed freely, weightlessly. How did they do that?

Distance helped me to understand the effects of the force field that my family's trauma had created. Like metal filings, we kids had lined up around the magnetic presence of the past and arranged our lives accordingly. I watched as my five brothers and sisters each went out on their own, attempting to cast off our freighted family legacy but mysteriously recreating lives that were arduous, edgy, lonely. I myself made extreme and often dangerous choices. Was it accident or irony that we were each in our own way reenacting the volatile climate of our parents' home?

I watched as my eldest brother Danny fought to free himself from the burden of his first-born son status and the imposed mantle of Talmudic scholar that came from my mother's side of the family. He left the Yeshiva world to study and teach Classics and Biblical Criticism. But academic life did not satisfy him. I saw him choose a Buddhist path and enter a rigorous and isolating Zen monastery. And I watched my parents, incapable of coping with his choices, cut him off.

I saw my older sister Shulamith emerge as a wildly talented writer and thinker who seemed to have inherited Dad's high voltage. As a small child, I looked on as she noisily threw off our parents' orthodoxy, defying its rigid requirements for women. She bridled when our father insisted that she make Danny's bed.

"Why should I do *that*?" she asked incredulously.

"Because you are a girl. That's what girls do."

"So? I will *never* make a boy's bed!" Shulamith screamed indignantly and stormed out of the house.

As a teenager, I watched as my sister's rage at this patriarchal world fueled her rise to a feminist visionary writer. Shulamith lived an incandescent life, rising and falling like a fiery comet. Quickly burning out and retreating into isolation, she did not wait for our parents to cut her off; she cut them off first.

Rejection and the silent treatment ran through my family's life like a disease. My sister Laya and I took our turns being cut off when we fell in love with nonJews. Our two younger brothers, who of our parents' six children chose to remain in the Orthodox Jewish world, followed their lead in breaking ties with some of us who had left the fold. All of us were on a fervent, sometimes dogmatic, search for meaning.

For a time, trying to breathe and discover my own life, I too, went underground, distancing myself from my entire family. I had left Judaism when I left my parents' home, casting off the burden of my birth religion like a heavy wool coat in spring. Free to wander, I traveled through Europe searching for unmediated spiritual experiences in whatever form I could find them. And I had plenty of company; there was an entire generation of spiritual seekers out there on a similar journey.

But try as I might to escape my fraught post-Holocaust upbringing, by way of distant travels, an interfaith marriage, and immersion in alternate spiritual paths, I came back to claim and reclaim my connection to my ancestral tradition. Finally entering formal studies, I tapped the ethical and mystical core of Judaism that I had never before understood. I received rabbinic ordination within the liberal Movement for Jewish Renewal in 1992. In retrospect, I realize that it was never Judaism that I had rebelled against; it was the unintended repercussions of unhealed trauma that I was attempting to flee.

Despite the astonishing lengths that I went to in an effort to deny it, I discovered that my ancestors were incontestably alive within me—with all their foibles and fears. And just as my grandparents' values had coiled down the twisted ladder of their DNA to me—love of learning and the written word, community, and yes, heavy food—so had the pain and injury of being a Jew.

A Container for Grief

Returning to Judaism, I began to understand the ways in which Jewish tradition itself supports recovery and renewal. My own family's responses to its Jewish trauma were admittedly extreme. But many of the ways Jews have dealt with historical trauma have promoted resiliency. The centuries of discrimination and scapegoating that stain Jewish history could have been fatal determinants, utterly paralyzing future generations. But this did not occur.

There have been many noble efforts by which Jews have moved their community *mai-Shoah l'tekumah*, from destruction to renewal, as Israeli Jews will tell you. We see these proud efforts in the memorials, museums, and monuments by which to remember and decry the racial hatred that methodically destroyed six million, and to ensure that the world would never forget their memories. We see them in the Holocaust Studies programs, archives, literary journals, and Jewish concentration camp tours, which serve as insurance policies that we not forget.

My own studies helped me to appreciate the psychological health of the Jewish religion, in which memory is sanctified and trauma is memorialized. For Jews, the cycle of the year, and even time itself, are seen as sacred. Each year there are fast days commemorating momentous days of destruction, the most auspicious one being the Ninth of Av, which falls at the apex of summer. This is the day of mourning for the Holy Temples in Jerusalem and other subsequent national tragedies.

Holocaust Remembrance Day, honored each spring by Jews the world over, is another powerful descent into sacred memory. On that day in Israel—known as *Yom HaShoah*— the memorial sirens blare, traffic stops, people get out of their cars and stand in silence; schools, businesses, and sports events come to a dead halt for moment of silent remembrance.

One can also find psychological soundness at the individual level: Jews traditionally sit *shiva*, seven days of mourning that begin after the funeral of a loved one. During this week, the secular world is suspended. Pictures are taken out and old letters are read, memories are plumbed, and stories are told. Friends come to listen and serve the grieving. The following year, on the specific date of our loved one's death, we light a *yahrzeit* candle, remembering them with good acts and the recital of the Mourners' Kaddish. And on holidays five times throughout the year, Jews say *Yizkor,* a memorial liturgy for those who have died.

To a secular Westerner, this may sound like an extreme emphasis on death. But notice that all these practices occur at specified times on the calendar. Memorial days start at a specific time, usually at sundown, and end at nightfall of the following day. So too, the effects of descending into the world of memory have a beginning and an ending.

Containment is one of the important functions of a religious community. And while community is an important ingredient in the work of healing trauma, anyone—with or without others—can adopt the practice of containment. It is based upon the principle of allowing grief, yet putting boundaries around our need to remember and mourn.

───────── *Steering Our Destiny* ─────────

Yet even with all of our ancient tools and noble efforts, Jewish historical trauma is not completely undone. For many Jews, catastrophe remains an unconscious organizing principle, an internal representation of reality that is still passed from generation to generation, wittingly or not. Our ancestors' past rears its head in the marketplace and in war rooms, on the battlefields, and at home with our children. Like stowaways who hide beneath the decks of our ship, painful memories go below the radar of our conscious minds yet whisper their secrets, drag and drain, compel and command us.

The power of the unconscious is mighty and requires of us immense vigilance if we are to steer our own destiny. Jews and all peoples who have suffered the traumatic effects of degradation and displacement, racial oppression and violent persecution simply for being themselves, must wrestle with their legacies. The past can become cause for fatalism, hypervigilance, and a sense of radical unsafety in the world.

But if we pay attention and do the hard work of facing what has happened, mourning our losses, and loosening the grip of automatic behaviors that follow a traumatic history, we can change our fate. Our injuries can ignite a passion for a new kind of identity, a new kind of life, one that courageously faces the humiliation of our own suffering and places it within the larger context of the world's plight.

Today, an increasing number of people are saying *No!* to the undertow of their life's tragedies. They are survivors of trauma who are not willing to be delimited by the events of their past, who refuse to consent to a post-trauma diagnosis, who want to go beyond an identity of victimhood. Forever changed by their tragedies, they are not looking to return to their old lives. They wish to move forward, to live in the world free of the constraints of trauma's consequences.

This is the journey I will be tracing in the chapters to come. Our first step is to understand some of the characteristic psychological roadblocks that both individuals and groups suffer in the aftermath of extreme trauma.

CHAPTER TWO

Trauma, Mind, and Body: The Paradox of Survival

FROM BIRTH ONWARD, we are subject to shocks that overwhelm us— unwanted advances on our physical boundaries, a drunken driver careening over the curb in our direction, violence breaking out on the street, the sight of death. Such experiences—when our sense of safety in the world is broken—remain with us, recorded in our psyche and in our nervous system. And whether we are talking about relatively common personal threats like these, or trauma on a massive scale, I have found that understanding the inner workings of trauma is key to recovery. In this chapter, we will see how each of trauma's hallmarks is designed to keep us in the game of life.

Central to all the ways we have of adapting to overwhelming experiences is one central component: our survival. Whether it's an individual on the street or an entire ethnicity that has been targeted with cruel social discrimination, research shows that the sequelae of trauma—both the immediate physical symptoms of trauma and its long-term effects on the body and psyche—are mobilized by our deep instinct for self-protection. Like animals, we are simply hardwired for survival.

It's ironic then that for both individuals and groups, the very strategies that initially protect survivors of trauma don't really help in the long run. In fact, behaviors that are most common, like isolating ourselves, becoming hypervigilant, and numbing ourselves against overwhelming feelings may actually perpetuate rather than spare us and others further injury.

Here we begin to see the inborn complexities that attend the healing journey after trauma. Paradoxes inhabit every step of the way. The brilliant psychological and physical mechanisms intended to keep us safe and defended against further trauma can become the very systems that lock the trauma in place. Let's take a look at Lena's story, one that illustrates individual, family, and intergenerational traumas, to explore some of these incongruities.

The Right to Go On Living

When Lena first contacted me for a counseling appointment, she told me she was thirty-two years old and needing help with a "spiritual dilemma" that was keeping her stuck. Opening the door for our first meeting, I found a slightly built woman with pale skin and beautiful green eyes. I immediately noticed how physically fragile she seemed; her bearing was that of a young child. But there was also a depth of wisdom in her remarkable eyes.

During our early sessions I learned that Lena was an artist whose art degree had not taken her far. She worked several odd jobs, and got by with some help from her family. She described a host of physical symptoms including insomnia, allergies, poor digestion, and episodic asthma, all of which kept her feeling wiped out. Although she came from an intact family with parents and two siblings who seemed to care about her greatly, she also suffered from extreme social anxiety and had broken off two potentially serious relationships.

Telling me her history was clearly uncomfortable for Lena. Her eyes avoided mine and she had a habit of grabbing the throw pillow from the corner of the couch and hugging it tightly against her torso as if to barricade herself.

"I just don't know if I'm meant to be in this world," Lena said in a near whisper at our third meeting. Then she lifted her eyes and furtively looked at me, as if to make sure I had heard her. I saw panic in her eyes.

"What gives you that idea?" I asked steadily.

"I've always felt that. Since I was little, anyway."

What could be behind such a statement? I wondered.

When I invited her to say more, Lena told me that her family had been in a car accident when she was seven years old.

"I was sitting in back so I was totally fine. But my cousin Theo was in front. He took the blow. We were the same age, best friends. He died in the hospital a few days later."

Lena was now staring off into the distance. Then she mumbled:

"It should've been me; I shouldn't be alive."

Lena had never healed from this early trauma. Like so many children do, she took on the blame for a fateful event she had not caused, nursing her guilt in secret. I imagined that the adults on the scene were themselves so devastated with their loss that they were unaware of Lena's need.

For the next several months, Lena and I worked together on her early trauma. With the use of EMDR (Eye Movement Desensitization and Reprocessing), an extremely effective tool for overcoming trauma imprints from the past, Lena seemed to be making progress processing her memories from the fateful collision. Layer by layer, we unpacked and examined the shock and terror of this experience and the beliefs she derived from it as a child. Over time, Lena came to an understanding that the meaning she had assigned as a little girl to the loss of Theo—a terrible mistake that was her fault— was not rational, and that she was not to blame.

But even with progress, Lena had a fey unworldliness about her. When I asked her what brought her joy in life, she got that faraway look again and just shook her head limply. Life is not about joy, her body seemed to be saying, it's about survival. Like a baby who cannot take in nourishment even when it's offered, Lena was failing to thrive.

It became clear to me that Lena had few friends. When people got too close, she simply cut them off. She preferred to be alone, she explained, and to use her spare time to make art. I could see that her instinct to isolate herself for self-protection served to perpetuate the inner shame and self-doubt that she carried, making her situation all the more difficult.

And Lena's self-protection extended to me. When she felt that she had overly exposed herself she would call to say she couldn't make our next session. Then I would wait to hear from her, sometimes for weeks.

———— *Uncovering Ancestral Trauma* ————

After one of her long absences, I was alarmed to hear Lena use the word *sacrifice* several times. She seemed to be hinting at something. Was it a fantasy of suicide? Then she brought in a dream:

> The scene is cold and dark. A prehistoric figure with big blocky stones up his back is there and he wants me for something. He wants me to climb his back. I am supposed to die up on top. It is like a scene from Rodin's *Gates of Hell*. There are many small people, like from a *shtetl,* clustered together at the feet of the figure. *The closer you are to death, the closer you are to us*, they say to me. The prehistoric figure looks at me with the eyes of my grandmother.

Lena's attraction to death took on another dimension that day. In addition to her family's car accident and the loss of her cousin, she was carrying the onus of another wound, one that predated her. We began our descent into what I call "ancestral trauma."

I asked Lena what her association was to the people of the *shtetl,* a small Jewish town in Eastern Europe. She responded with her family's story. Lena's maternal grandfather had lived in the Ukraine, in a *shtetl* called Tluste, she explained. When World War II broke out in 1939, the Jewish population of Tluste was less than 1,200, having been decimated by Polish and Ukrainian violence under the Soviets.

Life got much harder when the Germans took control in the summer of 1941. Her grandfather had been a prominent doctor and a man of means before having to move into the Tluste ghetto the following spring. During the next two years, the atrocities became unbearable. The ghetto had swollen with Jews from outlying areas. Disease was rampant. Lena recounted a particular Gestapo action in which 2,000 Jews were rounded up and escorted to the Tluste cemetery, where they were all shot. Several of her family members were among those murdered.

Lena's grandfather tried to escape with his wife and their small baby. They found a farmhouse several kilometers beyond the town and paid the Ukrainian farmer to hide them in its crawl space. But after a few weeks, the place proved too dangerous; they feared being given away. The doctor went off scouting for another refuge, which he found. When he returned, he discovered his wife and child brutally murdered. "His wife's name was Nadya," Lena told me, "Even though I never met her I consider her my grandmother. I'm sure those were her eyes looking at me in my dream."

For the next nine months, her grandfather hid in a loft above a stable. When news came in the spring of 1944 that Russian forces had liberated the region, he made his way back to his hometown, took in the devastation there, and then escaped to Poland with forged papers. There he met an old family friend from Tluste, who became his second wife, Lena's maternal grandmother.

But Lena most identified with her grandfather's first wife, Nadya, and the *shtetl* people of Tluste who had died in the mass grave. The question that Lena had tacitly expressed at our first meeting reverberated: *What right do I have to live— let alone thrive—when others have been robbed of their lives?*

Her ancestral story reinforced the childhood trauma that had lived at her core for so long.

This, then, was Lena's spiritual dilemma: Did she have the right to go on living? In both of her family tragedies, the fateful accident in which she lost her cousin, and the murder of her grandfather's people, Lena identified with the lost victims. The trauma she carried was complex; it was both personal and collective, intimately her own yet also belonging to her tribe. And on both counts, Lena was besieged by survivor's guilt.

——————— *Finding the Mother Lode* ———————

Trauma often stores itself in layers, not unlike the sedimentations found in an archeological dig. With attuned treatment and a safe environment, the psyche reveals itself one level at a time. It is common for more personal and current injuries to show up first, then the older, more ancestral strata to come into view. Most important is the through line, a common vein of meaning that runs through all the layers, a resonant theme that vibrates with emotion when tapped. This is the mother lode, and if one can find it, healing may be on the horizon.

In Lena's case, the accident in her early years had established a core belief that she was not meant to be alive and did not belong to this world. Why in fact, would you *want* to stay in such a world? This voice seemed to whisper in her ear constantly: this is a place where cruel mistakes happen (like the death of Theo), where life is utterly random, fallible, and not to be trusted.

We had clearly uncovered one cause of Lena's spiritual dilemma, but even these important insights did not go far enough. At the crux of Lena's failure to thrive was a much larger ancestral wound, one that lay in the bedrock of her family's history. And although it had been told in story form for decades, the tragedy that her grandfather had lived through and the rupture it created had been passed down through two generations without ever being fully mourned or integrated.

Recounting family tragedies is important, and, as we saw in the case of my own family who kept secrets, it is far better than keeping them hidden. But ultimately, mining the deepest levels of the psyche cannot be done with words alone. This is a territory rife with profound feeling, touching upon our existential core, our place in the world.

It was time to descend to a new layer of work. Now I understood the gravity of Lena's statement when she told me she did not know if she was "meant to be in this world." The pull she felt from the *shtetl* people and, most importantly, the invitation to climb the back of the archaic beast and place herself on the altar of history were all reiterations of Lena's core wound, demanding her fidelity. Being loyal to her deceased loved ones, in her mind, meant sacrificing her life to join them, not taking steps to make her life happier.

It is not possible to describe Lena's process in fine detail here. However, I can say that our work took a turn at this point, entering an interior world evoked by her dream, in which her ancestors were very much alive. In a series of sessions that were more akin to ritual and meditation than conventional therapy, Lena called upon her relatives. One by one, she invoked Nadya, then her grandfather, and finally, her cousin Theo. Lena addressed each one and listened in turn, engaging in a dialogue with her ancestors that was, for her, entirely real.

In the course of these extremely emotional conversations, Lena discovered that it was not at all the desire of her family or the villagers that she give up her life to join them. They looked upon her, rather, as the current embodiment of their highest hopes and aspirations; they both needed and wanted Lena's happiness and fulfillment on earth. Most important-ly, they promised their support and asked Lena to call upon them whenever she felt stuck.

In the months following these dialogues, Lena began to turn the corner in her healing journey. The fragile, childlike qualities I had noticed at first gave way to an increasing-ly full-bodied, grounded woman. Even Lena's voice became deeper and more resonant. She reported that she was sleep-ing better now, and had not noticed any asthma symptoms. She took up yoga at a nearby studio and began making a few friends. In time, she made meaningful contact with other art-ists in town.

I learned from Lena how trauma can freeze us in time. As Holocaust scholar L.L. Langer has written, trauma "stops the chronological clock and fixes the moment permanently in memory and imagination, immune to the vicissitudes of time."[1] Now it was as if someone had reached in and released an emergency brake that had been set decades—and even generations—earlier. With the support of her ancestors, Lena was ready to join the world.

Hallmarks of Trauma

The psychological burdens of a family's historical traumas often fall to the most sensitive of the new generation. In Lena's case, both of her siblings were high-functioning individuals, one a school administrator and the other an attorney. They too were aware of their family's history; this was a family that valued communication. But it was Lena who was most susceptible to carrying the psychological imprint of tragedy, possibly due to her early trauma at age seven, and to her inborn temperament. Both may have set the stage with elevated levels of stress hormones that accompany high-alert situations.

Clinical studies demonstrate how, once a neural pathway is activated by a high-intensity situation, subsequent stressors, even milder ones, will travel along the same pathway, reinforcing the connection and triggering heightened reactivity. Later stresses can also reactivate memories that were laid down under similar conditions. This is one of the reasons that once we have experienced a traumatic event, lesser stresses can be experienced as a return of our trauma.

Lena's case highlights other important characteristics of psychological trauma as well. Let's take a look at four of the most common ones, while keeping in mind that all of the ways we humans adapt to devastating experiences are rooted in our essential instincts for survival. So while each of the following trauma adaptations may keep us safe for a time, they may also paradoxically perpetuate the problems caused by the injury.

1. Dissociation

At the core of trauma in all its many forms is dissociation. This term—coined by Pierre Janet, the French psychiatrist who greatly influenced both Freud and Jung—is used to describe the psychological phenomenon of splitting off or numbing ourselves in the face of experiences that are too overwhelming to assimilate.

Many of us have experienced dissociation personally. If you have ever witnessed a terrible accident or received some bad news, you may have found yourself automatically putting your feelings on hold to keep your head about you. Dissociation buys us time to go for help, find safety, or get the privacy we need to feel our feelings. This splitting response, which is also called emotional or psychic numbing, is a completely normal defense mechanism.

In extreme cases, dissociation can be lifesaving because it seals us off from experiences that might otherwise shatter us. But dissociation demands a high price. If we go for too long without integrating what has occurred, our split-off feelings and memories will demand a way back into our consciousness.

I first learned about dissociation from psychiatrist Robert J. Lifton who conducted pioneering research on the Holocaust, Hiroshima, and Vietnam. In his staggering post-war interviews with Nazi doctors, he found that these men could only perform their ghastly, inhumane experiments by creating a "second self." Lifton called this process *doubling*, an extreme form of dissociation, which allowed these men to adapt to evil and betray the medical oaths they had taken to heal and not harm life.

Lifton also found that doubling was widespread among the victims of Nazi atrocities, who had to psychically split themselves into two in order to survive. Those who lived through the hell of concentration camps often reported that they had shut down their personalities in order to bear the unspeakable hardships, saying in some form: "I was a different person in Auschwitz."[2]

Healing from such extreme dissociation takes time and devoted work. It cannot occur until the traumatized "second self" is reintegrated into the personality. The struggle is to reunite the split-off parts into a single self, to bring the numb self back into full feeling and awareness.

I saw this in a woman I will call Kelly, who from age eight to ten, endured bullying and sexual molestation by her older half-brother. "When this happened I went into a kind of fantasy world," Kelly explained, "it was my escape...I would float away into this beautiful field of horses where I was a horse and I felt totally free and happy. I forgot all about the abuse for many years."

At age nineteen, Kelly started to have flashbacks. "It was like another part of me began poking through a wall. I started to have all kinds of painful feelings, and seeing scenes of what I had gone through. Sometimes my body would start to go numb and I had to slap myself to stay in the room."

Kelly had so completely removed herself from her physically inescapable situation that she created a second reality. In this way, she preserved her sense of wholeness until she was capable of dealing with what had happened. Her overwhelming feelings and sensations had disappeared into a kind of deep freeze, but they were never totally gone.

And whether we are talking about extreme protracted trauma or a single situation that overwhelms our coping mechanisms, the problem with dissociation is that part of us disappears. Our life story has inexplicable blank spots, and at times we don't know where our responses are coming from. We cannot be fully present with others either.

Another patient, Melissa, described her boyfriend, who had recently returned from his third tour in Afghanistan. "It's like he falls into a black hole," she said. "He just checks out without any warning. When he's like that I can't reach him, no matter what I do or say."

Dissociation is the means by which a person under threat disappears emotionally and mentally. In the moment of crisis the mechanism of splitting saves us. But if we do not do the hard work of reintegrating the traumatic memory fragments that have split off from our consciousness, we risk becoming increasingly disconnected from ourselves, our lives, and others.

2. Hyperarousal

In contrast to dissociation, in which our emotional responses are dampened or numbed (hypo-arousal), the hyperaroused state occupies the other end of the spectrum, where we are intensely focused and alert.

Hyperarousal occurs naturally when we encounter a real or perceived danger. Our bodies quickly become flooded with stress hormones like adrenaline and cortisol, which provide us with an immediate burst of energy and power.[3] These fight-or-flight hormones have one objective: they activate us to respond swiftly to life-threatening danger—to outrun a lion or

39

fight off an assailant. But when we continuously undergo traumatic stresses—as in a war zone, on dangerous streets, or in abusive relationships—we *remain* chronically activated. Then our stress hormones linger and circulate in our body for too long, keeping us hyperaroused, and ultimately becoming toxic.

As an unchecked residue of trauma, hyperarousal can take a serious toll on the nervous system, spelling adrenal exhaustion, insomnia, extreme moodiness, and difficulty simply taking life in. When high stress becomes a way of life, not only do our stress hormones stay elevated, but the neural pathways that tell us the world is unsafe get reinforced, thereby training us to stay in high arousal.

We find ourselves constantly scanning the world for danger, acquiring a kind of tunnel vision that narrows our focus. Our capacity to relax and take in simple pleasures becomes strained, and we are more likely to become activated by everyday stresses, especially ones that recall our original trauma. The phone ringing late at night, the sound of a police siren, the sight of blood, or even a traffic jam can trigger cold sweat, breathlessness, or a thumping heart, all signs that our sympathetic nervous system—which signals the release of our fight-or-flight hormones—has been triggered.

Most of us have experienced hyperarousal at one time or another. Think of a time when you had difficulty scaling down an inner sense of urgency or haste. Or as Terry, a high-powered investment analyst, described it: "Lately everything feels like an emergency. Any minute the shoe is going to drop, and I feel like I'm running for my life."

Occasional periods of high stress like this are inevitable. It's when we get habituated to a state of hyperarousal that problems are afoot. Being flooded with fight-or-flight hormones, our neo-frontal cortex begins to shut down, leaving behind our capacity to think analytically and embrace nuance and paradox. In this state, the world looks black and white; we tend to shoot from the hip, to speak and act with less awareness of others, and to be reactive rather than reflective.

The first step to stabilization is to find a safe place, a comforting relationship, or techniques that help us lower our state of arousal. Whatever means we have of slowing down the velocity and vibration of our lives will help to interrupt the neuro-biological patterns of hyperarousal: being in nature, yoga, meditation, swimming, and deep breathing are just a few. Once again, with steady, dedicated work we can make inroads into a survival mechanism that is no longer saving us.

As I have said, people who have endured trauma in the past or have "inherited" stress responses from earlier generations can be activated more easily. Here, we are touching upon the remarkable research emerging from the relatively new field of epigenetics (to be discussed below), which demonstrates how environmental stresses may be passed down inter-generationally.

3. Isolation, Avoidance, and Shame

Another hallmark of trauma, highly visible in the case of Lena, is the tendency to isolate socially. Withdrawing from a noisy world after a trauma is understandable, because once the startle response is set on high, ambient sounds are louder and it is difficult to filter environmental stimuli. I have heard many trauma survivors report that even walking down a busy street or shopping in a mall can feel unbearable. The choice to keep quiet and to oneself may seem like the kindest, safest strategy. After all, it's easier to rely on oneself than others; our own space seems like a refuge where we can be in control.

But while it may be innate for us animals to go into our cave to lick our wounds, prolonged isolation can feed the shame and self-doubt that often follow a traumatic event. Isolation can also perpetuate the sense that we do not need anyone, or that no one can understand or help us. Without exposure to new experiences and relationships, our traumatic memories get more fixed and inflexible, more resistant to change and integration.

Lena's self-isolation was reinforced by another post-traumatic coping mechanism: avoidance. She got herself into therapy, but often missed her appointments. She talked about her accident, but avoided my eyes, as well as her uncomfortable feelings, at least at first.

Another patient, a college student I'll call Marianne, avoided contact with her friends after she was assaulted sexually on campus. She simply cut them off without disclosing what had happened to her. "I felt so much shame. I figured everyone knew and blamed me for letting such a stupid thing happen." By the time she came to me, Marianne was thinking of dropping out of school. Once she opened up in therapy and spoke of the incident, allowing me to witness her pain, she began to hear that her "thinking" on the issue was irrational.

Avoidance comes in many forms. I have known clients who, in the aftermath of trauma, tell long stories that are completely unrelated to the overpowering pain they hold inside. Others minimize the severity of their experience by saying things like: *But what am I complaining about? Nothing like what people endured in Auschwitz!*

The problem is that avoidance doesn't work in the long run. In fact, it strengthens our shame and fixates our fear. In the end, survivors of trauma must face the critical events of their past, learn to stay present with their difficult feelings, and examine the beliefs that their experience has engendered.

Trauma, especially involving interpersonal violations, can rip away our self-confidence and thus, our ease with others. Allowing another human being to hear our pain, witness us as we tell our story, and remain in relationship with us after knowing what has happened to us is all-important. Rebuilding our trust in others is a critical component in healing and integrating our trauma.

For this reason, it is very beneficial to form a therapeutic alliance with a trauma-informed person.[4] This might be a rabbi or minister, trusted relative, therapist, or spiritual mentor—someone who can listen well, and gently help to reveal avoidant areas without pushing, always respecting that avoidance exists as a mechanism for self-protection.

4. Repetition

Finally, we arrive at one of the most puzzling hallmarks of trauma. I've said that humans are hardwired for survival, and that survival demands that we become hypervigilant to any signal or situation that recalls our original wound. And yet trauma survivors often place themselves in situations where their trauma will be repeated.

You might be wondering: Why would anyone ever choose to revisit or reenact horrific events? But remember that we aren't *choosing* consciously, because when we are traumatized we are not "master of our own house." These apparently compulsive reenactments may be due to the "blind spots" created by dissociation.

One tragic form of repetition is revictimization. We now know that once a person has been victimized, they are more likely to suffer the same or similar kinds of trauma. For example, studies show consistently that victims of rape are more likely to be raped again, and women and children who were physically or sexually abused as children are more likely to find themselves in abusive situations as adults.[5]

But the unconscious repetition of trauma can also be a major motivator of violence to others. Research shows that past victimization fuels perpetration in the future.[6] Most hardened criminals have histories of being abused earlier in their lives, and traumatic maltreatment in childhood approximately doubles the probability of engaging in many types of crime.

Likewise, numerous studies show that victims of sexual abuse often go on to victimize others.[7]

Patterns of repetition and reenactment may sound uncanny at first. But think of soldiers who reenlist and return to the battlefield after their tour of duty is done; victims of incest who become prostitutes; victims of domestic violence or trafficking, who, once rescued, return to their batterers—or find a new partner who begins the cycle again; male survivors who identify with their aggressors and do to others what has been done to them. These trauma survivors may be chasing some kind of resolution and comfort, but instead, they find further pain and self-hatred.

Freud theorized that the drive to repeat trauma was not under our conscious control at all. He believed that the aim of the "repetition compulsion," as he called it, was to revisit the traumatic situation in order to resolve or gain mastery over the experience. But clinical studies show that such mastery rarely occurs, and that people seldom make conscious connections to their earlier injuries. As neuroscience demonstrates, the part of the brain involved in compulsive behavior is separate from the centers that choose, plan, and integrate meaning. It is only when there is conscious understanding that the need to reenact the trauma is diminished.

And so the search continues for a better understanding of traumatic repetition. Some explanations focus outside the individual, on the toxic environments created by poverty and social degradation. Others draw on neuroscience research, which suggests that the answer may be physiological, as well as psychological.

Recall that after a trauma, stress hormones remain in the system, continuously generating what feels like a state of emergency, keeping a person on high alert. This kind of hormonal dysregulation often results in a terrible dance between feeling numb or split off (dissociated) and being ultra-mobilized and over-sensitized (hyperaroused). Functional magnetic resonance imaging (fMRI) shows that stress hormones in people who have been traumatized spike quickly and disproportionately in response to even mildly stressful situations. All of this leaves a person less in control, relying heavily on past behaviors and the well-worn neural pathways that make habitual patterns reflexive.

Getting Hooked on Trauma

After completing his duty in the Israeli Defense Forces, Kobi was bored and listless. Many of his friends went abroad to travel, but he chose to stay behind. "I was always on edge and couldn't enjoy myself," Kobi told me. "After getting out [of the army] it was like being in withdrawal from drugs or something. I was hooked on the rush that comes with army service and had to have more. I am ashamed to say it now, but I loved feeling all-powerful. I couldn't get enough of it." Shortly thereafter, Kobi enlisted as a career officer and served until physical problems forced him to step down.

Indeed, we might understand trauma reenactment as a kind of addiction. This repetition can elicit a kind of *analgesic effect*, meaning that it provides relief from our pain and anxiety. In this way, we can literally "get hooked" on trauma, because hyperarousal is so seductive—boosting energy, increasing strength, heightening the senses, and creating immunity to pain—for a while. These endogenous, or self-produced, opioids can act like morphine in the system, giving us a sense of self-mastery, or even pleasure. But like a drug, the effects of repetition ultimately fade, leaving the traumatized individual to feel, once again, helpless and out of control.

We can see how this cycle of numb/hyperaroused/out-of-control feelings flies in the face of rational choices and prevents the integration and healing of trauma. But breaking out of the cycle and resolving trauma *is* possible. It requires much dedicated work and a variety of new approaches, as we will see in Part II.

The Epigenetic Factor

Deepening our understanding of trauma's impacts, is the fascinating research coming to us from a field called epigenetics, which shows that while extreme stress does not change our DNA, the basic structure of our genes, it *can* affect how genes behave, or are "expressed" in the body. One focus of epigenetics is the chemical changes or marks upon our genes, a process called methylation. (Hence, the field of epigenetics: "epi"—outside or upon—and "genetics"—the genes.) These marks seem to affect the function of the gene itself.

The methylation process potentially allows us to adapt to both our inner and outer environment. And most important for our discussion, some epigenetic changes can be passed on to our offspring. Clinical studies give us evidence that stress and struggle can imprint itself not only on us, but upon future generations. The science of epigenetics shows that a person can carry evidence of their parents, grandparents, and even great-grandparents' social history. If, for example, a person's grandparents lived through starvation, deportation, or ethnic persecution, their descendants may show propensities to similar stress responses, both physical and psychological. Sometimes the similarities between generations are uncanny.[8]

I learned to appreciate epigenetic findings through animal studies. In one study at Emory University,[9] mice were exposed to acetophenone—a smell akin to cherry blossoms—and then received an electric shock to their foot. In true Pavlovian style, the mice became fearful and froze whenever they came into the presence of the smell, even when they received no shock. More importantly, their offspring—even the grandpups of the original mice, who had never met their grandparents or been exposed to the smell or shock—showed panic in the presence of acetophenone. The transmission of this environmental information, researchers said, was the result of epigenetics.

"It's not just recognition of a smell that seems to be transmitted down generations," McGill University geneticist Moshe Szyf said, describing the results of this study as unprecedented and startling. "It's connecting the smell with the fear response."[10]

Human evidence emerged from ongoing research into the survivors and descendants of the Dutch "Hunger Winter" of 1944-45, when the Nazis cut off deliveries of food and other vital supplies. It was expected that the children born from mothers who were pregnant at the time would be affected—researchers knew that starvation in the womb led to metabolic disorders. The surprise came later, in the 1990s, when the grandchildren of those starving mothers were also found to have higher rates of obesity and heart disease.

Even more relevant is the ongoing work of Dr. Rachel Yehuda, professor of psychiatry and neuroscience at Mt. Sinai Medical Center in New York City. Yehuda's research shows that gene expression and regulation produced by the extreme stress of life in the Nazi camps may have been transmitted to subsequent generations.[11] In a 2015 study of Jewish Holocaust survivors, she found that survivors' children proved to be three times more likely to develop a PTSD disorder if exposed to traumatic events than demographically similar Jewish individuals whose parents had not suffered in the Holocaust.[12] Overwhelming trauma, Yehuda said, "resets and recalibrates multiple biologic systems in an enduring way."[13]

Epigenetics can be complex to understand for nonscientists, but some scientists and writers are masterful in their portrayal of the science. Journalist Dan Hurley describes the process of methylation like silt that has been deposited on the cogs of a finely tuned machine after the seawater of a tsunami has receded. In much the same way, our experiences and those of our forebears are never really gone, Hurley explains, even if they have been forgotten. "They become a part of us, a molecular residue holding fast to our genetic scaffolding."[14]

Epigenetic research is still new, and as skeptics stress, epigenerational explanations need to be carefully applied to the intergeneratonal effects of trauma. And Dr. Yehuda reminds us that we have no way of knowing whether the epigenetic changes are linked to vulnerability or to residence.

Most important for our discussion is the approach taken by Yehuda and other scientists, who warn that even if it is true that trauma effects intergenerational changes, we *always* have the capacity to work with our biological realities. Knowing what our forebears went through helps us to better understand and have compassion for our family legacies and our own selves. Once we are cognizant of our history, we can better choose positive responses to our trauma legacies.

—————— *Through a Wider Lens* ——————

Jews are, of course, not alone as victims of historical trauma. In recent years, a new lexicon has cropped up—including cultural, historical, multigenerational, and intergenerational trauma—pointing to our growing awareness of collective trauma in the world, and the long-term effects of massive social violence. Dr. Yael Danieli is an Israeli-born pioneer in the study of intergenerational trauma legacies and editor of the *International Handbook of Multigenerational Legacies of Trauma* (1998). In this groundbreaking volume, she and her contributors explore the consequences of social traumas throughout the world, from the atomic bomb in Japan to the genocides in Cambodia, Turkish Armenia, and Russia.

Danieli's own work focuses on Jewish survivors of the Holocaust and their offspring, drawing on decades of records and clinical studies. She strongly counters the tendency within Holocaust literature to pathologize or overgeneralize. The Jewish trauma experience, like all cultural traumas, is not monolithic, Danieli insists. Instead, it can best be understood in family patterns,[15] which are not cast in stone. Freeing ourselves from our inherited family patterns is possible for both survivor and future generations. But this depends upon *awareness* of the trauma legacy that has been transmitted to us.[16]

Awareness, as we shall see, lies at the core of trauma recovery. And to grow our awareness requires finding a witness, both within ourselves and within others. We turn to this critical aspect of trauma recovery now.

CHAPTER THREE

The Importance of Being Witnessed

S URVIVORS OF TRAUMA OFTEN FIND themselves in
a double bind. On the one hand, there is an inner compulsion
to tell the trauma story and be heard, while on the other, there
is a sense that words can never encompass an experience that
feels beyond the limits of human ability to grasp. And so the
imperative to speak is often overcome by the impossibility of
telling, and silence prevails.

But with silence comes alienation. This is one of the reasons that survivors often feel as if they are "living in an alternate reality," as one client told me several years after being
sexually assaulted at gunpoint. After the trauma, she said, "I
felt removed from the world."

Orna, an Israeli tour guide who lost her daughter in a suicide bombing in Tel Aviv, also withdrew from life. For this
single mother, herself the daughter of Holocaust survivors,

the loss of her twenty-two-year-old daughter was shattering. Even in Israel, a tightknit society that has become primed to care for survivors of such a tragedy, Orna descended into a cave of isolation. "It wasn't a depression," she told me the following year. "It was that no amount of telling could come close to conveying what had happened for me."

Yet tell we must—eventually—because our stories are at the heart of human connection. After months of seclusion, Orna finally reached out to others, realizing that the twin needs—for quiet and self-protection, on the one hand, and telling and connection on the other—had to be honored. Indeed, if we can balance these two disparate drives, we may be able to build a bridge out of the seemingly impenetrable solitude that attends trauma.

Two elements are key: a safe witness and the ripeness of time. First, we need to find a person whom we can trust, a person who has the ability to receive our words with an open mind and no agenda of their own. With such a witness, we can create a safe place where the unspeakable can finally be spoken.

In Chapter One, I discussed the way a religious community and its rituals can become a kind of "container" for suffering by establishing safe boundaries around the mourning process. Here we have a different but equally important container, one that is created in relationship with an attuned and attentive person. With a compassionate listener, we enter a circle of safety where we can slowly begin to trust again. In this relationship, where we are truly seen and heard, we may begin to find meaning in our experience, and our humanity can begin to be restored after it has been stolen from us.

Even then, there are barriers to telling. Neuroscientists have discovered that trauma disrupts the very brain centers that enable us to assemble our splintered experience into words. Memory becomes fragmented, stored jaggedly in shards of image, sound, and sensory information.

The integration of these broken pieces often proceeds slowly. It may feel impossible to create a coherent narrative for ourselves, much less one that can be conveyed to another human being, no matter how sensitive they are. Yet it is the telling, and the receiving of our story, that is essential for trauma integration to occur.

Some survivors I have met maintain silence for another reason. They refuse to reduce their tragedy to an "official story," the kind of simplified narrative that translates easily into a news report or a sound bite. We don't want to turn our life into a press release. (However, some survivors develop just such a story for self-protection, so they have something to say when asked, "What happened?") Maya, whose son Tali was shot down in friendly fire over Lebanon while serving in the Israeli Defense Forces, refused to talk about the accident for months, feeling that to do so would betray his honor and the complexity of his life.

Again, timing was key for Maya. At first she rebuffed efforts to "get her to talk." She became ready on her own terms, and responded to her organic impulse to speak of her son's death cautiously, first with an older friend, then one or two more people who could listen fully, without haste or judgment.

But for Avi, the Holocaust survivor whose story is at the center of this chapter, it was more than three decades before he was ready to speak about his experiences as a child.

—————— *Cultivating the Inner Witness* ——————

When we "listen in" and attune ourselves to our inner experience, we develop what I call the *inner witness*. Connecting with ourselves may sound simple. But for people with a history of traumatic experience, cultivating the inner witness can be extremely challenging. Again, neuroscience may help us to understand why this is so.

Confronted with an inescapable event that overwhelms our coping mechanisms, our internal world becomes flooded with sensory information. This is because the prefrontal region of our brain goes offline—that part of us that normally assimilates incoming experiences, puts feelings into words, and gives us a sense of ourselves in time and space. Instead, the emotional brain (the limbic area and brain stem) takes over, and it is hardwired for speed and survival.

Signals from the limbic brain bypass the normal mediating centers that evaluate and judge our situation, to alert our system that we are in danger. Arousing our fight-flight-freeze impulses, they put us in a highly triggered state so that we can successfully outrun or deceive the lion at our backs. Perhaps unsurprisingly, these emergency circuits fire much faster than the neural circuitry in our analytical brain.

So while this state of high arousal may help get us out of harm's way, it also prevents us from objectively observing the situation at hand. Our ability to see, integrate, and store the incoming information is markedly reduced. So is our capacity to witness ourselves. These capacities will need to be reclaimed in time, after the emergency is over.

Restoring the self-witness was central to my work with Ken, a fifty-year-old sound engineer who came to therapy for sleep disturbance and night terror. Ken appeared at my door with a downcast posture in which I read self-shame. He had suffered from a series of on-the-job back injuries and his body was chronically tight and painful. Apart from his physical discomfort, he had very little awareness of his body at all.

During one session, I guided Ken into a relaxed state on the couch. Then I asked him to travel throughout his body with an imaginary flashlight, getting to know it from the inside and telling me what he observed. Normally talkative and articulate, Ken soon lapsed into complete silence, and was unresponsive to my voice. *Where had he gone?*

I could see his face grow pale, his breath quicken. He was unable to tell me what he was feeling, but to my eyes, he looked increasingly young and very terrified. When Ken resurfaced, he reported feeling disoriented and angry. In response to my questions, he mumbled some disjointed memories about a terrifying uncle, being left behind by his siblings, being afraid of the basement—all fragments with no cohesive picture.

Over the next months, we explored the dissociation that Ken described as his "black hole." He learned how to use his breath to calm his sympathetic nervous system when he felt himself "slipping away," and he added self-witnessing tools to his nightly routine: He consciously put aside his workday by focusing attention on ambient sounds and taking ten deep breaths. Before bed he charted his day in a notebook, paying special attention to his physical wellbeing. Although he still had nightmares, his sleep began to improve.

In our sessions together, Ken worked painstakingly to slow down the moments that he called "cliffs," where he seemed to be overcome with fatigue and lose all awareness. He learned that these sudden bouts of dissociation covered up important caches of information. It took roughly six months of devoted work until we were able to approach Ken's painful basement trauma. Staying mindful of his body's signals, not being frightened away by passing moments of nausea or spells of uncontrollable shaking, Ken bravely approached his fearsome childhood memories to witness and name the terror of broken boundaries and violation.

Over the next two years, Ken reoccupied his body in dramatic ways. A new vigor began to replace the timidity and shame I had first seen. His eyes, which had been furrowed and dull, now meet mine with a twinkle. Although Ken's therapeutic work continues, he now has tools with which to witness and care for himself.

Owning Ourselves

Trauma expert Bessel van der Kolk writes, "The challenge of [trauma] recovery is to reestablish ownership of your body and your mind—of your self."[1] When we *own* ourselves, we can visit our thoughts, feelings and sensations without becoming overwhelmed or dissociated. We have the inner tools that help us regain our self-awareness and equilibrium when triggers from our past pull us down a rabbit hole. Strengthening the inner witness is the beginning of self-ownership.

Cultivating the inner witness can be approached in a variety of ways: journal writing, the practice of yoga, mindfulness,[2] or other forms of meditation, and the body awareness techniques that Ken used are just a few. These tools calm the limbic brain, which is easily activated in those with trauma history. In turn, they assist in lighting up areas of the neocortex, the part of the brain responsible for insight, empathy, and self-awareness.

Importantly, the inner witness is the neutral observer who tracks our experiences with kind, alert attention. It is neither judge nor critic, nor even the problem-solver inside of us, but rather, the calm, self-aware part of ourselves that is wakeful, curious, and on our team.

─────────── *A Tiny Child Alone* ───────────

One of the most striking examples of the power of the inner witness that I have ever come across is the true story of a little boy, whom I'll call Avi, who endured the chaos of World War II on his own. Avi's astonishing capacity for survival was aided by a gift given to him by his wise mother, one that he used to create an inner witness.

After thirty-five years of silence, Avi finally told his story to Holocaust scholar Dori Laub as part of the Fortunoff Video Archive of Holocaust Testimonies at Yale University.[3] Although it is very painful to hear, the very act of telling it— and being witnessed by those who listened—produced profound healing for the man who endured the trauma.

As a four-year-old boy, Avi lived with his mother and father in the cramped quarters of the Krakow ghetto. The year was 1941. When rumors began to spread that the Jewish children in the ghetto would soon be rounded up for extermination,

Avi's parents began devising ways to save their son. Avi overheard them planning at night when they assumed he was asleep. Somehow they were going to send him away.

Late one night, Avi's mother wrapped him up in her shawl and handed him a tiny passport photograph of herself as a student. She whispered to him instructions and added that whenever he felt the need to connect to her, he should look at her picture. Both parents promised him that they would come and find him after the war and bring him home. Then, while the guards were distracted, Avi's parents managed to slip their little boy out through the ghetto's gate.

With his mother's photograph and an address scribbled on a slip of paper, Avi was on his own in the darkened streets of Krakow. The address he had been given was that of a brothel, hospitable to a homeless child because it was itself a marginal institution. Avi was received with open arms and given a glass of milk to drink. From the goodness of this precious drink and the kindness that was shown him there, he remembered this house of women as a hospital.

But eventually this refuge became too vulnerable, and Avi had to leave. A tiny child alone on the streets at wartime, Avi was utterly occupied with the task of survival. He joined other gangs of boys and intermittently found sanctuary in the homes of kind gentile families. In moments of solitude he would take out his mother's tiny photograph and talk to her.

Once, Avi took shelter with a family who provided him with the papers of a child who had died. This Catholic family had a custom of praying together every evening. As the family knelt and prayed in front of the crucifix, the mother of the house, who may well have guessed that Avi was Jewish, allowed him to pray as he wished. He would take out the small photo of his mother and pray to it saying, "Mama, make this war be over and come and take me back as you promised." Avi did not doubt his parents' promise for a moment.

Miraculously, Avi's parents survived the hell of the concentration camp. Perhaps it was the promise they had made to their son, or their own inner images of their little boy that helped them to persevere. After the war they found Avi and stood before him: now a haggard man and woman in shabby striped uniforms as if returned from the dead, ashen and gaunt, with teeth hanging from their gums. To Avi, they were wholly unrecognizable.

This is when the external reality and Avi's internal image collided with such force that he could not address the people before him as anything but Mr. and Mrs. His parents' return spelled the demise of his internal witness and the saving refuge that it had provided. It was only then that Avi began to fall apart, to feel the crushing weight of what he had been through.

In the absence of a true witness, Avi had used his mother's photo to create a virtual witness. This enabled him to survive the years that he spent on the streets of Krakow. It also allowed him to maintain a sense of his own selfhood as he struggled to navigate a chaotic and traumatizing world, and to create a coherent internal story—with a past and a future—about what was happening to him.

To survive in this world and find meaning in our lives, we need to be seen, heard, and witnessed. Attachment theory suggests that our sense of ourselves is created in infancy. An infant needs to have a bond with someone—whether a parent or caregiver—in order to develop socially and emotionally. This bond is the foundation on which the self is built; our healthy development depends upon it. Being seen and held in infancy creates the ability to see and hold ourselves later in life.

We can assume that Avi had received the gift of survival from his loving parents in the first four years of his life. His secure attachment to them and the passport photo of his mother helped Avi to endure what might have been unendurable to others. His vital bond to his parents was reflected and energized by the face on the photo. Such a tiny emblem was vast enough to save a young child living as a fugitive in the midst of a great war.

Avi's story shows us that even when we have no one physically there to witness our reality, it is possible nevertheless to find an interior witness, by using our inner capacity for reflecting and imagining. When we lose our sense of being adequately seen and held, as Avi did at the end of the war, it becomes far more difficult to face the horrors of life.

The Search for Invulnerability

Ironically, it was only after being reunited with his parents, that Avi's inner suffering began. He began to have a recurrent nightmare. In his dream, Avi found himself on a big conveyer belt that moved him closer and closer to a metal compactor. Utterly powerless, he could do nothing to stop the vicious machinery that was designed to crush him to death. Inevitably, Avi woke up in a panic.

The war now over, Avi was still a little boy rejoined with his mother and father, yet he was anything but a child. He had no way to integrate his wartime trauma, and without an inner-witness, Avi could not face the horrors he had been through. So he adapted himself to the external world, where being out-wardly tough and manly was both useful and praiseworthy.

As soon as he could, Avi found his way to Palestine, and joined what would later become the Israel Defense Forces (IDF). There, he became a high-ranking officer known for re-peated acts of bravery in which he heroically risked his life to rescue comrades under fire.

But Avi never considered his behavior to be in any way ex-ceptional or brave. His heroic acts were simply part of the in-vulnerable self-image he had constructed. He had successfully suppressed the abandoned child-victim part of himself. And like many survivors, he tried to convince himself that his trau-ma had never happened, and that even if it had happened, he was not affected, as if he had "walked under the rain without getting wet."[4]

In 1982, thirty-five years after Avi had come to Palestine, Dr. Laub asked him to be interviewed for the Fortunoff Video Archives. This invitation provoked an internal crisis for Avi, and he refused. In all those many years, Avi had never spoken of his history to his wife or his children.

His wife asked him, "Why don't you think it over? What are you afraid of?"

He answered, "I am scared that everything will come back."

"You've been living with this thing for thirty-five years af-ter the war and you're still afraid," she said. "You never talked about it. Why don't you try the other way?"

Finally, Avi agreed. Before the interview he stayed up all night in deep distress, talking with his wife. Finally, in the morning he fell asleep. Once more the nightmare returned, but this time it was different.

"It was again the rolling presses," he reported to Dr. Laub: "It was again the feeling of helplessness and of terrible anxiety. But for the first time in my life I stopped the conveyer belt. I woke up still feeling anxious but the anxiety was turning into a wonderful sense of fulfillment and satisfaction.... I feel strongly that it has to do with the fact that I decided to open up."[5]

Avi finally uncovered his painful secret story, and he was heard. For the first time since the war, he allowed himself to feel his fear, vulnerability, and his excruciating past. But he was no longer alone. Now the world was his witness.

Let us be clear: The telling and hearing of Avi's story did not erase his Holocaust trauma. Nor did it give him back his childhood, or undo the horror of what he had been through. Yet a deep inner strength began to emerge for him—not the military strength he had built up, but rather, a private kind of heroism.

Taking the step to being witnessed also produced an exhilaration and freedom in Avi, and for the first time, he understood the extent to which his burden—and his silence—had shaped his entire life.[6] He had come home to himself at last, to connect the two halves of his personality that had been estranged from each other—the lonely, traumatized child and the war hero. He was finally able to integrate his trauma, and stop the monstrous machinations of his inner world.

Unseen and Unheard: When the Witness is Lost

It is here that we begin to turn the corner from the singular experience of individual trauma to that of larger groups like families and entire ethnicities. Being witnessed is perhaps just as critical at a collective level as it is for individuals. And large groups suffer from the same characteristics of trauma as individuals do. In both, recovery and resiliency depend not only on material aid, but on being seen, heard, and witnessed.

Something deep in the psyche shifts when we know we are not alone. Without human eyes and ears to share in our reality, our suffering can become meaningless and unbearable. This is one reason that many survivors of the Holocaust lost all hope in life despite their physical survival. For in fact, the world outside had turned a blind eye to their plight, apathetic to their suffering.

And there was another loss, too, one that transcended even human indifference. For roughly twenty centuries, Jews throughout Europe had endured relentless persecution. Again and again, they had rebuilt their communities after banishment, forced conversions, and annihilation. For all that time, Jews had largely maintained their faith in a god who cared for them, an overarching divine intelligence whom they believed witnessed their suffering.

Only after the unspeakable atrocities and methodical evil of the Nazi regime was faith in a guiding and providential principle crushed for many Jews. How was it possible that the Chosen People could be so utterly abandoned by their god? How could God have turned a blind eye to their inconceivable suffering? It was this divine abandonment that gave rise to a psychospiritual crisis of vast proportion.

In the terms of this book, we might say that there was an unprecedented loss of the *divine witness*. That is, the seeing, loving, divine protector who had watched from on high, whose presence had forever given meaning to Jewish history, had ostensibly vanished.

As Jews were being raked up from the ends of the continent for methodical, industrialized extermination, it seemed that both God and the entire world had turned away from their catastrophic fate. Indeed, war archives closed to researchers for seventy years have only recently revealed the extent of the silence.

It was widely assumed that the Allied leadership discovered the scope of the Nazis' mass murder only when they liberated the concentration camps. We now know that they suppressed or ignored this information for at least two and a half years.[7] As early as December 1942, the British, American, and Soviet governments were well aware that so far two million Jews had been murdered and another five million were at risk, records reveal. Nevertheless, none took immediate action.[8]

Here, Jewish history becomes paradigmatic of history as a whole. What do we make of the radical indifference of the world as it beholds the extreme suffering of others? How do we understand villagers who looked on as their Jewish neighbors were stuffed into cattle cars? That after arriving in free waters, ships filled with refugees were turned away from port, sent back to a sure death? Such denial is surely a form of collective dissociation, one that continues to paralyze us to this day.

Yes, the Nazis went to extraordinary lengths to conceal their crimes, using every tool of bureaucracy, intimidation, and propaganda to delude the world. Even so, attempts were made to bear witness to their savage methodologies. Diaries were written and buried for safekeeping, photographs were taken in secret, testimonies of escapees and other messengers were given in the free world. Why did all of these efforts fail? Perhaps the sheer extremity of the Nazi atrocities was beyond the human cognitive capacity to perceive and digest.

As Dr. Dori Laub, who dedicated himself to recording the testimonies of Holocaust survivors like Avi, later wrote: "The degree to which bearing witness was required entailed such an outstanding measure of awareness and of comprehension of the event—of its dimension, consequences, and above all, of its radical *otherness* to all known frames of reference—that it was beyond the limits of human ability and willingness to grasp, to transmit, or to imagine."[9] Or, as scholar Shoshana Felman pointed out, death became "radically *indifferent*: everyone is leveled off, people die as numbers, not as proper names."[10] Even the inner witness cannot survive such radical indifference.

Like so many perpetrators of racial persecution, the Nazis capitalized on a world numb with disbelief, all the while they succeeded in convincing their victims of their otherness and their unworthiness to live. This is how victims of persecution gradually become complicit with the victimizer: by becoming deluded into the false "truth" of their own sub-humanity. One psychoanalyst who treated survivors put it this way: "Hitler's crime was not only the killing of the Jews. But getting the Jews to believe they deserved it."[11]

As I had experienced in my own family, for decades after the liberation of the Nazi death camps, there was a frozen numbness, indeed, a collective dissociation regarding the atrocities that had occurred. And for many, this numbness was compounded by a profound shame for not having fought back, for the means by which they survived, and for the mere fact that they were alive when so many innocents had perished.

The price of silence is high, as we have seen. Oppression and its residues of shame, rage, and frozenness stay with us and within us. So do the alienating effects of not being witnessed. These traumatic residues have the power to distort our self-perception and even to become the organizing principles in our lives that are passed down to our offspring.

Yet hope lies in the act of witnessing. When we find ways to wake up from the numbing effect of death's indifference, when we testify to evil and bear witness to others, we are reversing the process of genocide's inhumanity. The eyes that see and recognize such acts are the eyes that have the power to restore humanity.

CHAPTER FOUR

Awakenings

HEALING FROM TRAUMA CAN TAKE years, sometimes decades. But I have heard many trauma survivors report experiences, sudden turning points on their journeys, and new realizations that radically changed their orientation to life. These unanticipated shifts, when a fresh and often broader perspective suddenly became clear, allowed the individual not merely a return to functionality, but increased freedom from the confining effects of their trauma, and an ability to step into a new way of living.

However we explain such shifts in awareness—serendipity, grace, or just psychological readiness—they amount to changes of heart and mind that bring with them new lines of reasoning and relief from the automaticity of trauma reactions. For some, their new outlook followed a series of events. For others, their awakening was radical and occurred nearly

instantly. In this chapter, I'll describe several of these remarkable turning points, which I have drawn from the stories of
survivors I have worked with as a psychotherapist or have interviewed as a researcher.

——————— Saying No to a Living Death ———————

My quest to understand more about trauma recovery in
Jewish families took me to Israel. Sadly, trauma can be found
everywhere in the Jewish state, and I found many who were
willing and eager to tell me their stories. Because the country
has been at war since its inception and before, everyone who
lives in this tiny land has lost loved ones: sons and daughters,
teachers and students, comrades in arms, relatives, and friends.

Yet Israeli culture is far from morose. It throbs with life
and vitality.

"Life goes on," Daniela told me the first time we met. "It
must. There is so much loss here. I think the whole country
would grind to a halt if everybody stopped to feel their pain."

I had traveled to visit Daniela where she currently lives,
in a sleepy town nestled in the hills between Jerusalem and
Tel Aviv. It was eighteen years earlier when she and her husband Boaz received the news of her eldest son's death. Tom,
a combat soldier serving in Lebanon, was twenty-one when
he died. He was killed in a massive air accident when two
Israeli military helicopters crashed into one another. There
were no survivors.

Daniela recalled her initial state of shock and dissociation. "I was honestly somewhere else," she told me, "I wasn't
here. But the *shiva* itself"—the Jewish seven-day period of

mourning—"I remember as a very holding experience. People came, good friends, and many others whom I didn't even know. We were never left alone. Day after day, people filled the house.

"But one day some people from the kibbutz came, including two or three older mothers who had also lost their children, mostly in the Yom Kippur War. I remember one key moment when one of these old mothers came up to me and whispered: '*You see me? I look alive. But I am not alive. I died with my son.*'"

Even then, something in Daniela recoiled at this woman's dark proclamation. "This was very hard for me to hear. I knew I did not want such a fate! At that moment, I said to myself: *I will either live or I will die, but I will not agree to a living death.*"

Her eyes filled with tears as she continued and she looked away. "Of course, it didn't change all at once. There were times I just wanted to die. I didn't want to go on living."

We sat in silence for a few minutes. Then Daniela smiled at me, and shrugged, perhaps a little embarrassed by how much she was revealing. I met her wise, hazel eyes and noticed how her face was lined with history; her thick dark hair shot through with grey.

"In the first year I had many dreams," Daniela continued. "Some were about Tom coming and telling me things. Sometimes I could see him in the grave. Sometimes he came as a little boy. And once I dreamt of giving birth to a baby girl whose body was distorted and crippled. She couldn't move. I somehow knew that crippled girl was me. After this dream I realized: *If I go on like this I won't make it. I am poisoning myself with anger and hatred.*"

I had heard other parents speak of being lost in a morass of anger and hatred after losing their children to senseless violence. The loss of a child is one of the most traumatic life experiences, and many parents fail to recover. When the loss results from a vicious act of hatred or from a terrible mistake, as in Tom's case, the mourning is all the more complicated.

But for Daniela, the ominous comment of that older bereaved mother had proved decisive. She was presented with a stark choice: *Go on living as a ghost or find your way to a new life.* She initiated meetings with a wise friend who was skilled at interpreting dreams. Over the next several years, she found the guidance and strength that helped her recreate her life. Exactly ten years after Tom's death, Daniela published her dreams in a book and dedicated it to him.

Daniela's decade-long journey was aided by her astute intuition, which told her that her dreams and strong feelings were important signposts that could guide her toward healing. Stopping to explore, rather than pushing aside or suppressing the "irrational" signs and messages that come our way, can prove extremely helpful. When we learn to trust our inherent or "felt" sense about life, we find that we have a deeply embedded instinct that provides us with valuable information.

Like radar on a ship, such bodily messages and dreams as the ones Daniela experienced, can steer us away from approaching danger and toward channels of healing. Listening inwardly in this way, Daniela learned how to navigate away from the "living death" that many Israeli parents experience after losing their sons and daughters.

Like other Israelis I have met, Daniela's face shows the lines of history. Yet she is vivacious and has an easy, contagious laugh. She meets regularly with other parents who are suffering traumatic losses similar to her own, offering them the benefit of her wisdom, coaching them to find their own moments of awakening.

─────────── *What We Left Behind* ───────────

Esti was thirty-five when she came to see me upon the recommendation of her internist, who suspected an anxiety disorder. She and her American husband Steve had suffered three miscarriages before their daughter Shiraz was born. They named her after the ancient city in Iran known for its gardens, where Esti's great-great-grandparents once lived.

Esti was born in the United States near the end of 1983, shortly after her parents and maternal grandparents had fled Iran. Her parents had told her the story of their narrow escape many times, how her father Yakub had paid an exorbitant amount in cash to drug smugglers who knew the desert routes and were used to running opium and human cargo across the border. She had also heard her mother Raqel tell the now legendary family story of walking out of their magnificent home in Tehran with nothing but a shopping bag, leaving all her beautiful clothes and furnishings, and simply closing the door behind her. Raqel was pregnant with Esti at the time.

By the early 1980s, life for religious minorities at the hands of Iran's revolutionary Islamist regime had grown untenable. Although Esti's family was well aware that Jews caught trying to escape the country risked imprisonment or execution, they were highly motivated. Her maternal grandfather, a successful businessman in Tehran, had been tipped off by a Muslim neighbor who was a member of the Iranian Revolutionary Guard, that he was in line to be arrested, and his assets seized. Less than a week later, Esti's parents, along with her mother's parents, Rahim and Pari, fled the country in which they had lived for generations.

As if she herself had made the journey, Esti told me how her family rode in a cart down narrow winding dirt roads seated on bundles of opium. Entering the Pakistani border town of Quetta, the family found their way to a plane to Karachi where they stayed for a few days with the help of another Jewish family. Another cash bribe to a Pakistani officer got them on a flight to Switzerland, and after several months, they obtained asylum in the U.S., ending up in Miami.

Esti told her family story with pride. Her anxiety was focused on another matter: how to help her seven-year-old daughter who suffered from recurring night terrors and separation anxiety. Day after day, Shiraz would cry herself into a state of collapse and was unable to stay in school. Her highly driven parents worried about her falling seriously behind.

After several fruitless visits to her school counselor, as well as ongoing weekly sessions with a child psychiatrist, Shiraz's situation did not seem to be changing. I had the sense that Esti's little girl was what family therapists call the "identified patient," the family member who enacted the distress lurking in the larger family system. There was more to this family's puzzle to discover, and luckily, Esti was a curious and highly motivated client.

About two months into our work together, I pulled out a large pad of paper and a box of colorful pens and sat next to Esti as I showed her how to map out her genogram. A genogram is similar to a family tree but includes more information about the relationships and interactions of family members. It can also contain health and disease patterns, reasons for death, and major separations between family members. I hoped that the genogram would be a useful tool for Esti to identify patterns of behavior and emotional relating in her family that went beyond her, her husband, and her daughter, where the problem seemed to be residing.

Esti drew Shiraz as a pink circle at the bottom of the page, with herself and Steve in the line above her. As she filled the paper with circles and triangles signifying her various family members, it became clear that she knew little about certain parts of her family story. In particular, her father's side of the tree was vague and incomplete. Would she go back and ask him for more details?

The following day I picked up a frantic voice message from Esti. Her father had flatly refused to answer her questions. Her mother had looked at her in terror and broken down completely. Could she bring her mother in to see me?

Esti's mother Raqel appeared in my office the next day and sat next to her daughter on the couch. Raqel was elegantly clad in a silk turquoise suit and matching scarf, but her face was dour and her red eyes were downcast. Both she and her daughter looked as if they were in a state of shock.

"What has happened?" I asked.

"For all this time I thought I knew the whole story," Esti practically wailed. "Papa always told us his parents were gone long before they left Tehran. Now I hear that his mother was still alive in '83. She got left behind. Can you believe it? They simply left her! How could they do such a thing? I have not stopped crying since they told me."

Esti's grandmother, Yakub's mother Sarah, had indeed been left behind. She was ninety-two and blind by then, and although she was mentally sound, they knew her frail body could not endure the hard trip. Fearing that the vociferous old woman might alert her caregivers to their departure, Yakub and Raqel had slipped away without telling her their plans or even saying goodbye.

This revelation was followed by a time of great mourning for Esti's family. Yakub and Raqel's profound shame, and their well-kept secret of more than three decades, was finally out in the open. Over the next months, photos were brought out and much grief and pain were uncovered. Esti's sessions with me often alternated between tears and expressions of rage. She insisted that the family create a memorial ceremony for her grandmother Sarah who had died in Tehran in 1984. They were happy—almost relieved—to comply.

Yet something else was emerging in our sessions. Even as Esti passed from disbelief to shock to rage at her parents, followed by grief and mourning, her daughter Shiraz was mysteriously growing stronger. Her parents had told their little girl only the general outlines of the family story when she asked what all the tears were about. But they had left her out of the highly emotional memorial service.

Esti reported that Shiraz was growing "carefree," like other seven-year-olds in her class. Over the next several months, she began going off happily to school, making friends and having play dates. It was as if this little girl had been carrying her family's hidden family wound. Shiraz's collapse and fear of abandonment—like an echo of her great-grandmother's heartbreak many years and thousands of miles away—had been healed.

Here is a case in which a tragic family separation was buried, seemingly too overwhelming to be felt or told. But the traumas of guilt, grief, and abandonment were destined to resurface in some form, and they reemerged in the unconscious of the younger generation. Fortunately, the wound came to light before Shiraz's separation anxiety became so engrained that it disrupted her social and psychological development.

Dislocation and family ruptures—an inevitable byproduct of war and civil strife—are occurring in exponential numbers today. With these wounds come the personal traumas of disconnection that scar families. Facing such injuries and deeply mourning the losses is critically important. When they are left unfelt, our pain simply goes underground, reemerging wherever it can find an opening, then pushing to be dealt with. As we have seen, this often occurs in the generations to come.

—————— *As If Seeing for the First Time* ——————

My research in Israel brought me to Rami, a seventh-generation Jerusalemite who was in his mid-fifties at the time of our talks. Rami had fought in the 1973 Yom Kippur War and had lost many of his best friends during that time. Emerging from the war angry and bitter, Rami told me, he had one goal in mind: to detach himself from the pain and concentrate on his own life and interests. In this clear and quite conscious act of dissociation, Rami blocked out his pain just to move on with life.

"Then," Rami said," on the fourth of September, 1997, just a few days before Yom Kippur, my bubble was destroyed by two suicide bombers who blew themselves up on Ben-Yehuda Street at the center of Jerusalem. They killed five people with them that day, including three little girls. One of them was my fourteen-year-old, Smadar."

"It was a Thursday afternoon, the beginning of a very long, very cold night which continues until today," Rami said with a faraway look. "At first when you hear about [a terror attack], you keep hoping that maybe this finger will not turn towards you. Then gradually you find yourself running in the streets trying to find her, going from hospital to hospital, police station to police station.

"Many long and frustrating hours, until eventually very, very late in the night you find yourself in the morgue, and you see a sight which you will never ever be able to forget for the rest of your life.

"Then you come back home. The house is filled with thousands of people coming to pay respects for seven days of *shiva* and you are enveloped by these thousands of people, a very clever design to ease your way into a new kind of life. But on the eighth day? Everybody goes back home to their normal everyday business, and you are left alone.

"You have to wake up, to stand up and face yourself. And you have to make a decision: *What are you going to do now with this unbearable burden, with this new personality, which you never thought existed? What are you going to do now with this anger that eats you alive?*"

The hair on my arms bristled as he spoke, and I could feel tears building up behind my nose and eyes. Rami was speaking rapidly now. It was an interview on a fiery roll, and I didn't dare interrupt. "There are only two options," Rami continued. "The first one is obvious. When someone kills your fourteen-year-old little girl you are so angry that you want to get even. Now, this is natural, this is human. It's the way most people choose: revenge and retaliation. It's a cycle of violence that never ends.

"But then after a while, you think: *You know, we are human beings; we people are not animals, we can use our heads.* And you ask yourself questions like: *Will killing anyone bring her back? Will causing pain to someone else ease this unbearable pain for you?* Certainly not. So in a gradual and complicated process you come to the other option.

"Much more difficult!" Rami said with a sardonic laugh. "It took me almost a year, foolishly enough. I had to make sense out of this senseless thing. One [way] is sinking down and dying slowly, which is what happens to most bereaved families here. And the other is trying to find a reason to get out of bed in the morning."

In the midst of his personal dilemma, something happened that changed Rami's life. It was during the week of *shiva*, while mourning for Smadar, that a stranger named Yitzchok Frankenthal arrived, speaking about the need for peace.

"He was one of the thousands of people that came to my house during those seven days, and I was so angry then. I went crazy. I yelled at him: *How can you do it? Step into someone's house who has just lost a loved one and talk about peace! How dare you?* But we started talking and he told me about his son Arik who was kidnapped and murdered by Hamas in 1994, and about this organization that he created for people who had lost loved ones but still searched for peace, fought for peace.

"He was a religious Jewish man, you know, with a *kippah* on his head. You know how we tend to put people in drawers, judge them by the way they look, and especially by the way they dress? I was certain that he was an Arab-eater for breakfast, a fascist, and a right-winger," he said with another sarcastic chuckle.

"So how did you get over your anger?" I asked Rami.

"I got a little bit curious," he answered after a pause. "Frankenthal wasn't insulted by me. He just invited me over to watch a meeting of his group. And I said, okay. That was fifteen years ago."

Frankenthal's group, the Parents Circle-Families Forum,[1] is a nongovernmental organization composed of Israeli and Palestinian families who share the common bond of lost family members in the ongoing regional conflict. Frankenthal founded it the same year that his son Arik was murdered. He understood firsthand that traumatized parents need a safe social container in which to grieve their losses.

"I was standing aside, very detached, very cynical, very reluctant. And I was watching [people from Frankenthal's group] coming down from the buses, people that for me were patriots, living legends ... people like Yaakov Gutterman, a Holocaust survivor who had lost his son Raz in the first Lebanon War. [Gutterman] was one of the first bereaved fathers who had the guts to demonstrate against the evil war in Lebanon. I saw people like Rony Hirschenson, a close and dear friend of mine, who was known in Jerusalem to be a peace activist. Rony lost his two sons in the conflict.

"And then I saw something completely new to my eyes, to my mind, to my soul: the Palestinian bereaved families coming down from the buses, shaking my hand, crying with me." Here, Rami paused and closed his eyes, as if stepping back into the moment. Then he looked up. "I was so deeply moved and shocked.

"I was forty-seven years old at the time, and I am still ashamed to admit that it was the first time in my life that I met Palestinians as human beings. Not as workers for my people, not as transient people, not as terrorists, but as people who carry the same burden that I carry, as people who suffer exactly as I suffer. I remember seeing an old Arab lady coming down from the bus with this long, black traditional dress and she had a picture on her chest of a six-year-old girl exactly like my wife carries the name of our daughter."

In that moment, Rami's well-defined structures suddenly collapsed. Seeing his Jewish heroes together with ordinary Palestinian workers as intimate friends spending the day together brought him to a state of extreme cognitive dissonance that distressed and transformed him. Something woke up inside of him.

"That was the day I realized I could not go back to my old way of being, could not continue to take Smadar's death as a *fait accompli*, as the 'law of the land,' without fighting against the conditions that brought it about." Soon thereafter, Rami joined hundreds of other Israeli and Palestinian member families who are active in the Parents Circle-Families Forum.

"Look, I am not a religious person," he said. "I have no way of explaining what hit me back then fifteen years ago. But from that point on everything changed."

——— *Healing the Pain of Generations* ———

As Robert Jay Lifton has written, all survivors of trauma undergo a struggle, to give "form or meaning to an otherwise incomprehensible experience, and above all, to their survival."[2]

There is evidence, Lifton says, that the offspring of survivors must undergo a similar struggle. But because they are working with events that are physically removed from their lived experience, it is often like groping in the dark for clues. In my own practice, I have heard second- and third-generation survivors report feeling crazy, abnormal, and even mentally ill due to the trauma symptoms they internalized growing up with traumatized parents.

This was the case of Monica, a graduate student in her mid-twenties, who came to a Jewish ancestral healing retreat I led and later sought me out to tell me her family story in more detail. Monica was engaged to be married the following summer and she worried that her "irrational fear of abandonment" might taint their otherwise healthy relationship. Why did she always expect the worst? She had extreme anxiety, and often experienced a sensation of "deep dread" in her body, especially when she felt disconnected from people she loved.

Just days before, in fact, she had suffered a debilitating panic attack when her fiancé had come home a few hours late from an outing. She had fantasized a gruesome accident, imagined calling his parents with the news of his death, even rehearsed his funeral. "I'm always scared," she told me. "If I don't know where my loved ones are, I panic."

Monica had been extremely close to her maternal grandmother, Shirley, who had died two years earlier. "Even when we were young [Grandma] told us her stories," Monica recounted. How she hid from the Nazis in the forest for twenty-six months. How she saw her mother and sister shot dead in front of her eyes, and at the same time took a bullet to her own face. The soldiers left her for dead. We grew up with these stories."

Later, in graduate school, in a psychology project, Monica began researching her family more closely. "I found a video that my Uncle Harvey made of my grandmother four months before she died. As I sat there listening to her, I was shocked to hear her say these words: *I'm always scared. If you say you're coming and then you don't come...I can't take it. I expect the worst.*"

"I couldn't believe my ears. Those were my exact words!" Monica exclaimed. "The same words I used with Evan when he was late: *If you say you're coming and you don't come...I can't take it. I expect the worst.*"

"At that moment, I said to myself, 'Oh shit, my anxiety is so much bigger than me!' And ever since, I started noticing more patterns in my siblings and in myself. My sister has so much anxiety; sometimes she can barely leave the house. And all of us suffer from terrible self-doubt."

Monica's revelation energized her studies. She began looking into research on epigenetics and intergenerational legacies. Meanwhile, I began looking into the extraordinary facts of her grandparents' lives.

Radomsko, an old city in central Poland, fell to the Germans early in the war. Its resident Jews were immediately forced to move to a few narrow streets, one of the first ghettos ordered by the Nazi regime.

For the next two years, Polish Jews from twelve surrounding towns were transported to the Radomsko ghetto and squeezed into the gated streets, creating unbearable overcrowding. Jews were subjected to forced labor, beatings, theft, and arbitrary murder. Everyone twelve years and older was required to wear a large J (for *Jude*, Jew) on their clothes in patches of varying colors, signifying their utility to the

Nazis. Monica's grandparents, being young and able bodied, wore the yellow patch, meaning compulsory labor seven days a week.

In July 1942, with typhus and malnutrition raging, news arrived that trains had begun to transport Jews from the Warsaw Ghetto to Treblinka. Radomsko was next. There was panic. Some Jews built cellars in which to hide, others planned their escape. Shirley was among them. She slipped out of the Radomsko Ghetto and hid in the nearby Plavnov forest.

Separately, Monica's grandfather Albert also escaped the ghetto. A group of eighteen arrived to the forest in January 1943, and immediately set to work to build an underground bunker to survive the winter. At first they received bread and potatoes from a man in the Polish underground. When that failed, a forester took over feeding them in return for money.

In the spring, the group put up makeshift tents. They picked mushrooms and berries, and Shirley would sometimes sneak into nearby villages to steal bread for her mother and sister. Life was always tense.

In the winter of 1943-44, the group returned to their bunker and huddled down against the cold. Just before spring, they were discovered. Most of them were murdered, including Shirley's mother and sister, and Albert's girlfriend.

Shirley and Albert, two of the four who survived, decided to get married. They wed in May 1945, Monica told me. "They didn't know what else to do. They had no one else left in the world, and they didn't want to be alone. My grandmother didn't want to have children. But my grandfather convinced her that by building a family they could put the horrors of the past behind them."

Years later, Shirley began to tell the story of their escape to her children. But her husband Albert remained a closed book. He shut down, erupting with rage when he could not bear his feelings.

Just before Monica's wedding, as her family gathered from various parts of the world, I asked for the opportunity to meet with Monica's mother, Sue, and her uncle Harvey. They eagerly complied.

"What was the legacy your parents left you?" I asked the two siblings.

"*To fear everything!*" Harvey replied at once. "I was the product of my father's beatings. He did not know how to communicate with me, or anyone. He controlled us with his anger; our mother with her fear.

"And yes, I pushed back," he continued, "but despite my rebellion, I was extremely closed up. After Albert died in 1979, something led me to sign up with the Center Within in San Francisco, where they worked with Primal Scream [therapy]. I always had this lump in my throat, and finally everything started to come out. I cried every day for six months straight.

"I stayed with the center for fifteen years. I was like a bottomless pit of emotion. One of the center's leaders told me I was healing the pain of generations."

Both Monica's mother and uncle had taken the path of therapy and spirituality, becoming lifelong seekers. Like many second- and third-generation survivors I have met, their need to find answers to existential questions and to attain spiritual calm was paramount. Now in their sixties, Sue and Harvey still travel around the world, living in healing communities, following spiritual teachers, and working to heal their trauma legacy.

One last question haunted me. It was about the bullet that hit Shirley in the face. "How did she survive that?" I asked Monica.

"After shooting my grandmother and her entire family, the Nazis left her for dead. But of course she wasn't dead. Somehow the bullet lodged itself in her nasal cavity and it stayed in her face her whole life. She complained about a lot of things, but never about that. Strangely, it's my mom who has constant pressure in her face."

Moral Injury: The Trauma of Being the Bad Guy

The Israel Defense Forces (IDF) are considered by many Israelis to be the backbone of Israeli Jewish society. Army training and service is where lifelong bonds are forged, and for all intents and purposes, it is where young Jewish Israelis are initiated into the realities of adulthood. All Jewish Israeli citizens[3] over the age of eighteen are obligated to serve their country, men serving three years and women two. Until the age of thirty-five, Israeli men are called up annually for a month of reserve duty, called, *miluim.*

I contacted Avner, an IDF reservist, for an interview upon the recommendation of an Israeli friend who was interested in my research. The friend had simply said: "Talk to this guy. He has a story you need to hear."

Avner was happy to travel to meet me at my apartment in Jerusalem. He was a trim, twenty-nine-year-old Israeli with sparkling blue eyes, short-cropped hair, and a knit *kippah* on his head. As he sat down on the couch and launched into his story, I was surprised to hear him speak in flawless English.

Later I learned that both of his parents were Americans who had immigrated to Israel in 1967.

"I grew up in a family and a society that educated me to be a good person, to give *tzedakah* (charity) and to care about people who are less privileged than me. Not only my parents, but my teachers [modeled this]. I grew up Orthodox. So in my community in Rechovot, I was involved in the religious scouts and I was always involved in one volunteer group or another.

"That was simply what we did. It was seen as the right thing to do. And of course, when it came time to go into the army, that was seen as the right thing to do. And it *was* the right thing! Because that's what my dad did, that's what my brother did. Why shouldn't I? It *is* the *right* thing, it's our army; the epitome of everything we wanted to be, right? We were not the *Yehudi galuti* [the Diaspora Jew] but the *strong* Jew. This is what I wanted to be, of course.

"I could question the way I was brought up, but in my community, in my society, a good person goes into the army, serves his country. And the truth is that the exact same Avner who did his *shnat sherut* [year of community service] was in the scouts and volunteered for Magen David Adom [Red Cross]. The same exact person was a soldier. That was *me!* That's how I felt I was someone in the world. I saw the reactions from my family and community and I knew, oh yeah, that's a good thing to do.

"So I was a soldier, and suddenly I found myself in people's houses. Suddenly I found myself arresting children. Suddenly I find myself *wanting* to shoot the bullet and kill someone. That was *me*. It wasn't someone else.

85

"There were some friends in my unit that did some very bad things.

"For example, a guy [in my platoon] who would come in [to a Palestinian village] and destroy every house he entered. I didn't destroy every house, but I enjoyed the fact that *he* destroyed the houses. I enjoyed the fact that everyone [in our platoon] slept on the beds in the houses that we entered. It was just part of what we did."

Avner continued, as if thinking out loud. "There are a lot of aspects of the army which are good, but some are really bad. Specifically, talking about the power [soldiers] have, well, it's a corruptive power.

"You have this power as an eighteen- or nineteen-year-old. I had the power, and this is what I did: I'd enter houses at night and take over; put an entire family in one room; take away all cell phones; if they wanted to use the bathroom, they needed permission from us; if they wanted to use the kitchen, they needed permission from us; if they look at you the wrong way, you punish them. You can slap them; you can arrest them; you can take them with you. And this is only one practice that we did: entering houses. It's also the checkpoints, the searches; it's every practice in the [policy] of control.

"In that sense, if I think of trauma—and trauma is a big word but I will use the word—I had the trauma of being *the bad guy*. But understand, the main victims are the Palestinians. We are not the main victims. We are much more the victimizers. And that in itself is traumatic."

With those words, Avner stopped talking and coughed. Suddenly, he began to cough uncontrollably. I quickly left the room and brought him a glass of water. Finally, the spell abated. Avner closed his eyes for a minute to collect himself. Then he continued.

"I will give you a short story—because as Jews we tell stories—of this one operation outside of Nablus. I was sergeant of a sniper team. [It was] one of the first operations I led my troops in. It was me and another officer.

"Almost on a nightly basis we took over houses. Houses where people lived. We would just enter and set up our observation equipment.

"This one night we were getting closer to the houses we were targeting. And suddenly, there was somebody screaming. Sort of like a wounded animal, but with a human voice.

"It was coming from a house that had first-floor windows around it, and we realize the noise is coming from the inside of the house. We are scared that we will be revealed. Me and the officer take our guns. He smashes the window and we peer in with our guns, and what we see lying on the floor is an old woman, the age of my grandmother. Probably she was scared, heard us coming, and fell from her bed.

"We are peering in with our guns, with our helmets on. Then at the end of the hallway, we see the heads of her family members sticking out. They are petrified. They are scared to death of us. *Of me!*

"Me and my officer said: 'Shit, this is a fucked-up situation.' We both realized there is nothing to do here and we left. But I remember as [my men] went marching on, standing there in the outskirts of Nablus, saying to myself: *What the hell am I doing?* Like, *Who am I doing this for? How could this be a good thing?* Not on a philosophical level, but how could this be? I feel that this is totally bad what we just did.

"How could anyone explain to me that this was a necessity?" Avner exclaimed a little too loudly. "And I couldn't find an answer. I remember just standing there saying: *I want to throw my gun down, but I can't because I have soldiers and they count on me and my officer counts on me.* Which, by the way, is a very strong [motivator] which keeps you in the system. Your friends, your comrades, your position, your officer.

"That was a moment where I really felt [Palestinians] were looking at me as the epitome of evil. They were scared; there was hatred. But hell, *I am a good person!* I always wanted to do good things." Avner paused here. Then he continued. "There were a lot of those [moments], but that was one where the 'glass cracked' for me, you know, a little bit more. Or maybe it was just easier for me to realize how I am seen on the other side."

Avner told me that the moral dilemma he experienced that night only increased in intensity throughout his military service. He managed to fulfill his duty as sergeant and cautiously gravitated to other IDF soldiers who also felt wracked by the ethical conflicts and concerns provoked by their assignments in the Occupied Palestinian Territories.

The Israel Defense Forces do indeed defend Israel's citizens from concrete threats like terrorist attacks. But unlike its official name implies, Avner told me, its actions are not solely defensive.

The realization that IDF policies were creating an unbridgeable moral conflict in him and many others, tipped Avner into action. "The things I took part in are not things I am proud of. It's something I am taking responsibility for. There were a lot of moments that I remember, a lot of incidents that stuck with me. But the strongest feeling was [the clarity] that I was a soldier who did these things, and now I am a civilian. I am the same person in both. But now I have the right to say: *This is wrong.*"

Avner's harsh awakening is surely one that soldiers around the world must encounter. It is the realization that *you are no longer innocent.* The inner struggle to question and confront group behavior, and then to speak openly about one's moral conflict has been termed a "moral injury."[4] It results from having witnessed or perpetrated acts in the course of military service that one perceives to transgress moral red lines, often producing deep shame.

The injury to Avner's moral conscience did not go away. As he told me how his life had evolved since his army service, I recognized many of the same features engendered by other forms of psychological trauma: emotional numbing, hyperarousal, and especially, a tendency toward shame and isolation.

Fortunately, after his IDF service Avner found other like-minded reservists with whom he shared his experience. They became members of an Israeli organization called *Shovrim Shtikah*, Breaking the Silence, a group of veterans and reservists, both men and women, who collect and share testimonies about their military experience in the occupied Palestinian territories.

The organization's stated mission is to "break the silence" of IDF soldiers who return to civilian life in Israel and "discover the gap between the reality which they encountered in the [occupied] territories, and the silence which they encounter at home."

Unsurprisingly, there has been a wide array of reactions to Breaking the Silence in Israel. At times, the reservists' work has met with a grateful public, as when their photographic exhibit of the oppressive conditions in the occupied territories was displayed in the foyer of Israel's Supreme Court in Jerusalem. However, as Israeli society and government have moved to the right, Breaking the Silence has come under high-profile negative scrutiny.

Beginning in 2009, after soldiers who served in Operation Cast Lead[5] came forth with testimonies about their experiences fighting in Gaza, members of the organization have been called traitors for questioning the country's policies and engaging in activities that are purported to harm their fellow soldiers.[6] The Israeli government has castigated the group, calling it "an enemy that harms Israel."[7] The pushback against Breaking the Silence seems to strengthen the organization's members, who claim there is a widespread need for such an organization, one that allows Israeli veterans to deal with issues of conscience and moral conflicts that arise while serving their country.

Despite the negative response from the Israeli government, Avner has found healing within his new community. The moral injury he carried from his army service was transformed when he realized he was not alone. Linking up with fellow reservists who were suffering similar wounds to their conscience, he gained the strength to speak out about his experience of dissonance as a soldier who takes his Jewish upbringing to heart, to publically question widely accepted military policies.

Avner's activism became his road to healing. In 2017, he became the executive director of Breaking the Silence.

—————— *Subtle Moments of Choice* ——————

In each of these cases, we can identify a specific moment of demarcation in which a survivor opened up to a new awareness. At this subtle moment of choice, how we choose can quite literally determine the direction our life will take.

We might think of greater awareness as a thing to celebrate. As we have said, awareness is a fundamental ingredient in trauma recovery. But awakenings can also bring with them additional pain—whether through the truths they reveal, or because they signal a departure from community consensus, removing us one step farther from others. Nevertheless, these turning points present us with the possibility for growth.

Moments of new awareness like the ones we have visited are most often uninvited. They are a gift that we cannot simply will. But we can recognize them when they occur, and we can listen carefully. Whether they come in the form of an unwanted remark, a tidal wave of emotion, or a visceral sense that something is wrong, if we follow their lead, we often discover a deeper wisdom. I found this to be true in the case of my own family tragedy.

CHAPTER FIVE

The Terrible Gift

IT WAS THE END OF the summer of 2012. I was busy organizing my ideas for High Holiday sermons I would be delivering to my congregation the following month. One of my life goals had been to create a spirited community that embodied the compassionate values of the Judaism I had grown to love. Another was to understand how healing occurs after grave injury. For this, I had just returned to graduate school in psychology. My days were very full.

The call came on a late August morning. I had woken up with a weakness that day. My head seemed to throb in rhythm with a persistent ringing of the phone. Finally, I roused myself, picked up the phone, and heard my sister Laya's voice. *Tirzah? It's Shulie. She's dead.*

Our sister Shulamith had been found in her New York City apartment. The cause and time of death were not certain.

But one fact was: Like our eldest brother Danny, Shulamith left this world cut off from others. It had happened again; another one of us had died alone.

Danny had died decades earlier, a few days before my twentieth birthday. He had abandoned his academic career to pursue Buddhist studies and a rigorous life in the Rochester Zen Center. At that point, cut off by my parents for practicing *avoda zara*, idolatry, he had lost all ties with the family except for me, his kid sister.

Now here we were again: one more desolate death in the family. In the days following—as I wept over my failures to reach her, poured over old letters, and cobbled together dates—I saw with new eyes. It was as if flashes of lightning had suddenly illuminated the dark territory of my family's life. I began to discern the tragic pattern that was emerging from all of these tragedies.

Our parents—a refugee from Nazi Germany and a born-again Jew who had witnessed the liberation of the camps—had carried the charge of bringing to the United States a Judaism that had been destroyed in Europe. To them, it was the only authentic Judaism, an orthodoxy based on an uncompromising rabbinic system that demanded total adherence. As their children arrived—six of us over fifteen years—we were scooped up into the roles that they deemed would best fulfill this mission.

But in their rush to restore the lost world before the shock and grief of devastation had fully registered and been integrated, Sol and Kate had stepped into a kind of Jewish zealotry that bore its own brand of violence. There was neither time nor knack for the subtleties of parenthood, nor the understanding that every child has his or her own unique nature, which requires time, attention, and receptivity in order to flourish.

By the late 1950s, the Jewish community knew all too well about the horrors that had transpired in Europe, but they did not dare speak of them openly. Who could process the shock, let alone address the loss of a million innocent children, or the desecration of thousands of Torah scrolls? Instead, they poured their intensity into restoring a way of life that had been all but destroyed by the Nazis.

It was decided that Danny and Shulamith, their eldest children would be sent away to yeshiva in Cleveland for training. And in the years that followed, they were inducted into a rigidly structured religious world that demanded total devotion.

But faith does not come by will alone, nor by unyielding pronouncements of duty. Danny and Shulie, all of thirteen and twelve years old when they left home, suffered greatly from the absence of family belonging and parental warmth. They soon chafed at the parochial system in place at their schools.

At Jewish holidays, Danny would come home pale and dour looking, decidedly bookish and without laughter. Shulie would arrive ready for a fight. Her very nature reviled any system in which men or a patriarchal system wielded the upper hand. This wild young female with her flowing black mane was hardly a demure candidate for Jewish homemaking and mothering, for which she and her schoolmates were being groomed.

By the time she was twenty-five, in 1970, Shulamith had long since left our parents' home and the Jewish world. She had co-founded three radical feminist collectives, spear-headed numerous women's protests, and published her land-mark manifesto, *The Dialectic of Sex: The Case for Feminist Revolution*. Written at white-hot speed, the book railed not only at male privilege, but at sex distinction itself. It created a media uproar.

As Shulamith made headlines, our bewildered and exasperated parents withdrew into a strange combination of ignominy and pride. Our mother, privately thrilled at the prospect of having a famously published daughter, declared loudly that she would never read the thing. Our father laughed off *The Dialectic* as a "joke book." He began flaunting his favorite necktie covered with tiny pink pigs (an ironic choice of attire for a strictly-kosher Jew). Each little piggy was crowned with three almost imperceptible letters: MCP (male chauvinist pig), our father's proud adage for himself.

Pitted against our parents' plan and their strict, almost idolatrous commitment to Jewish law, was Shulamith's equally unwavering call for revolution against male oppression. This of course included their brand of Judaism, and the centuries of rabbinic interpretations of Torah that she insisted had subjugated women.

But the book's instant celebrity put Shulamith at the fore-front of a volatile and competitive political movement. In those early days, the radical feminist camp was restive and snarky. Eager to disown all forms of hierarchy, the women acted out with "horizontal hostility," and the founding leaders often came under scornful scrutiny. Shulamith was attacked for dominating, for "being defensive" and "unsisterly." She withdrew from the public eye and became increasingly reclusive, hiding out in her tiny East Village apartment, painting, writing, and reading; effectively sealing herself off from the clamorous world, including our entire family.

From the beginning, Shulamith and Dad had been interlocked like two sparring animals. Dad was Shulie's biggest adversary, never missing a chance to put her down. As a teenager, I remember his sarcastic tirades about her errant life, her choice to live in poverty with black people whom he called *"schvartzes"* and others of lesser ilk, and how she would never be fit for marriage. On her part, Shulamith railed at Dad's cocksure sense of entitlement, his unquestioned dominance in the family, his untested political views.

Suddenly, in 1981 at age sixty-five, Dad died. That was when Shulamith's mental health began to deteriorate and, ultimately, to collapse. Perhaps his sudden absence from the world left her without the ballast she required to ground her fight. In the following years, diagnosed with schizophrenia, Shulamith suffered a series of hospitalizations. She struggled with and resisted medication, and finally, withdrew from life itself. Devoted friends and family members made regular attempts to break through Shulamith's self-imposed barriers. Ultimately, all of us failed.

Her orthodox graveside funeral was a simple affair. Holding to Jewish tradition, it was organized hastily, in order to bury her as soon as possible after death. None of Shulamith's friends, followers, or colleagues were present. Just three siblings—Laya, Ezra, and myself—and a handful of local relatives were in attendance.

Brief words were delivered by Ezra, our black-hatted brother from Brooklyn. He reminisced warmly about Shulamith as his protective older sister, creative teller of stories that he still carried with him. But he knew little and spoke less of her brilliance or the cultural breakthroughs Shulamith had spearheaded. I attempted to add to Ezra's eulogy, about women around the world whose lives had been revolutionized by her work, my own included.

My words though, seemed to dissipate into the summer sky. The sun pounded down relentlessly. There were neither chairs set up nor a tent to shelter us. Just the deep trench, a pile of earth pierced by four shovels, the small huddle of family members standing together sadly, and our sister, being lowered into the ground in a simple wooden box.

──────── *What Death Revealed* ────────

What I finally understood was this: Shulamith was born into the still smoldering ashes of the war in January 1945, as Auschwitz was being evacuated and the Manhattan Project rehearsed its nuclear capability. Our mother had taken her and Danny to Ottawa, to live with her German-refugee parents, while our father served in Germany. When Dad returned later that year, his eyes were still filled with death. He had no room in his heart for his tiny children, no patience for their needs. Our mother too was numb and absent. Stumbling about on a new continent, she soon had a house clamoring with children. But her head was full of ghosts.

Danny and Shulamith, the eldest ones, suffered the full weight of our parents' raw and unworked post-war trauma, and both had died tragically. Now in the shadow of Shulamith's death, I comprehended just how a family's ancestral trauma rumbles through history like a train, depositing its load, car after car, into our newborn skin.

How could it be otherwise? We are porous beings, and children especially so. In a study called *Mourning and Longing from Generation to Generation*, Tamar Shoshan concludes that from the moment of their birth children are exposed to the traumatic suffering and "uncompleted mourning" of their parents: "Long before verbal communication, the baby absorbs the reflection of sadness, excessive concern or simply the parents' 'emotional absence.'"[1]

But as conscious adults, we have the capability to search, understand, express, and forgive. Shulamith's death had brought with it a terrible gift. The sacrifices that she and my brother made to find freedom gave me the impetus to go on my quest, to investigate the inner workings of psychological trauma and its passage, to stop the train before it reached future generations.

This, then, is the deep reason this book exists. My eyes had been opened to a pattern of isolation, cutoffs, and enforced silences that ran through the generations of my family. Suddenly, other mysterious pieces in my family puzzle arose to mind and fell into place: I have recounted Ziggy's treatment by my grandmother at the end of the war, her acceptance of him made conditional upon his practicing orthodox Judaism. But there were other stories. For example, there was the suicide of my mother's eldest brother, who had refused to become a rabbi, and the unexplained absence of my father's father, who I met only at the very end of his life, long after he was cut off from the family. All of these people had been, like Shulamith, deemed unacceptable and shut out from the current of my family's love.

With these realizations came a profound compassion for those who boldly struggle to free themselves from the strictures of conditional love, whether in a family or in a larger community. More surprising yet was the tender pity I found even for the castigators—my parents, grandmother, and others—who were carriers of belief systems they held more precious than love itself. I was learning how often hardened hearts were the tragic byproduct of wounds incurred long ago and never healed.

Looking at our families and finding within them traumas that beg to be known is a critical first step. Then there are choices that must be made, and crucial decisions that can disrupt the negative patterns that come down to us from family and tribe. How we go about transforming the legacy of our people's trauma is the subject of Part II.

Postscript

Our mother died in Israel early in 2015, after suffering from dementia in the final years of her life. The disease ravaged her, but it also softened her in some unexpected ways. She relaxed her normally terse and judgmental manner. She looked people in the eyes at length, told them she loved them, cried more, and suffered gravely over her losses and mistakes. For this reason, we had not dared to tell her about Shulamith's death.

On her ninety-first birthday I called to congratulate her. She was still living in her Jerusalem apartment at the time, surrounded by her collections of books, dolls, and ceramic art. She was having a good day, and our conversation was lively.

Then her tone changed. I soon realized that she was not speaking to me at all, but that she had mistaken me for

Shulamith, as she often did. What she said was so remarkable that I grabbed my keyboard and tapped away as she spoke. This is what my mother said to her eldest daughter:

"I want you to know that I am reading your book with great interest now. I appreciate your ideas and I appreciate your writing. It's a pleasure for me, and I'm proud too, that you were so independent and freethinking.

"Listen, I think I was wrong to the point that I didn't read the book.

I was not ready to read it with an open mind, and now I am, and I'm sorry that there were opinions that came into the way that couldn't be liberated.

"It must have hurt you so much. You were very much alone with your philosophy. I'm sorry that all those difficult years you suffered from alienation from the family. You didn't do anything wrong at all; it was your own way of deciding how you wanted to live, and I shouldn't have been such a stranger.

"It's late in the day to say this, but I say it with a very open heart now. I'm saying it was very wrong and opinionated to be so limited in my outlook that I couldn't see you. I couldn't be more sincere about this. It was wrong of me that I wasn't a freer thinker. All that time I was trying to educate and influence you.

"Now I am away from all those earlier concepts. I was too limited at that time to give you freedom. I cannot completely blame myself, but now I am reading your book the way it should be read."

My mother too, had had an awakening.

PART II

INTRODUCTION

The Principles of Jewish Cultural Healing

God remembers the sins of the fathers upon their children
even unto the third and fourth generations (Deut. 5:9).

As a child in Jewish day school, it unsettled me deeply to learn this line from the Hebrew Bible. What kind of God was that, I wondered, who couldn't lay down his grudges, even to the point that innocent children would be caught up in their grandparents' mistakes? And then to boast about it!

Decades later I came to understand that this verse was articulating a profound psychological truth. But it was getting lost in translation.

Words are like crystals. Many years later in rabbinical school, I studied hermeneutics, the Jewish art of interpretation: how to turn Hebrew words and phrases around, to study their many facets, and then to gaze again, until they reveal a resonant truth that holds meaning for today. Each word in an ancient verse matters, and how we translate each one can wound or heal.

The verse in question, for example, sounds ominous. Its common translation reads like a curse. But with equally precise scholarship it can mean something that many of us know to be true: *The mind of the universe observes the wounds of parents as they ripple down to their children, grandchildren, and great-grandchildren.*[1]

The Bible is simply pointing to a universal fact, one reflected in the many stories I've reported in Part I: The violations and heartbreaks that are suffered in one era often continue to travel through time, creating a legacy of new suffering until they are finally faced and felt.

─────────── *Turning the Crystal* ───────────

My research files contained the narratives of first-, second-, and third-generation Holocaust survivors; Middle-Eastern and Russian families who had suffered repeated religious persecution and exile; and Israeli Jews who had lost children in terror attacks or suffered moral wounds as soldiers in the Israeli Defense Forces.

Each of their stories was deeply personal and distinct, each a different facet of the crystal. What was said; what was not said. How the story continued the train of Jewish cultural identity; how it broke free into new landscapes of awareness. Journeys that crisscrossed the globe from Berlin to Shanghai,

Cairo to Miami, Kiev to Sderot; journeys that were suffered internally, without ever leaving home.

All of these personal accounts I understood to be *Jewish cultural traumas* because in each case, the suffering described in them was rooted in the narrator's cultural identity as a Jew. Turning the crystal again and again, I began to realize that the Jewish culture itself had been changed by the sum of these individual trials.

If individual trauma is a blow to the psyche that breaks through defenses with such suddenness and force that one cannot react to it effectively, then collective trauma is a blow to the living organism that is a community. Over time, a trauma-informed worldview may become embedded in the identity of the culture.[2] Because it involves many life experiences, the harm works its way into the awareness of a group slowly and even insidiously, bringing with it a gradual realization that the social fabric of the community no longer exists in quite the same way, that the body politic, the "we" of the people has been irrevocably changed.

"Sometimes the tissues of community can be damaged in much the same way as the tissues of mind and body," sociologist Kai Erikson writes.[3] Then the traumatic wounds inflicted on individual people "can combine to create a mood, an ethos—a group culture almost—that is different from (and more than) the sum of the private wounds that make it up."[4]

We see this happening in every direction today. The tribes and ethnic groups around the world that are suffering political and religious oppression, displacement, and ethnic cleansing are among the world's 68.5 million refugees. Continuously exposed to terror, homelessness, poverty, and unthinkable conditions, masses of Syrians, Central Americans, and Africans are reshaping the face of their own cultures. As their cultures change, so does the face of our global culture. The future that our children will inherit is shaped by the traumas of the present.

A New Culture Emerging

I began to see my transcripts and case studies telling a new yet old story, one of the latest iterations of Jewish culture emerging from the fires of collective Jewish trauma wrought by the twentieth century.

My stacks of interviews and case notes contained both sides of the Jewish cultural trauma legacy: stories of suffering that went on to produce continuous suffering, and testimonies of those who struggled to stop the train of their mistrust, hopelessness, and rage. I found in some narratives a determination so relentless that it would obliterate anything in the path threatening Jewish survival. Alongside these were narratives describing a fierce commitment to alleviate suffering everywhere, to *tikkun olam*, repairing the world.

The need to isolate, build walls, and declare self-sufficiency is, as we have seen, a strong component of a post-trauma profile. This tendency is not without its positive function. But although I witnessed the urge to build walls in many of the people with whom I worked, it was most evident at the start of their trauma journeys when they most needed protection. For many, the symptoms of fear and hypervigilance were eventually superseded by a growing sense of safety and trust in others.

I found that feelings of responsibility for and interdependence with others—not building walls or cutting others off—typically showed up as later signs of restored health after traumatic injury. Perhaps due to the point in their journey when I met them, their narratives evidenced a heightened sense of compassion for others, those who felt an innate responsibility to go out and alleviate suffering.

Erikson identifies this as a centrifugal pull especially common among trauma survivors: people who gravitate outwards, to help others who are suffering.[5] As we will see, Holocaust survivors and their offspring disproportionately tend toward professions in fields of medicine, social work, and clinical psychology, as well as education and scientific research. Concern for the wellbeing of others and the desire to spare others the pain they themselves had suffered was a leitmotif throughout my interviews.

Another dominant theme was the search for a larger meaning. These Jewish spiritual seekers often emerged from families with traumatic histories, fueled by discontent with the status quo and a fervent need for answers. Here the iconic work of Viktor Frankl informed my listening.

Frankl, the Viennese psychiatrist who used his own Holocaust experiences and those of his fellow prisoners to articulate his views, held that the human search for meaning has a "primary motivational force." "Each man is questioned by life," he wrote, "and he can only answer to life by answering for his own life."[6]

I myself had been such a seeker, and I have met Jews throughout the world, studying, traveling, residing in ashrams, zendos, meditation centers, and spiritual communities.

Many writers have noted that disproportionate numbers of prominent Buddhist and Hindu spiritual leaders and teachers were born Jews. This irony, and the fact that so many young Jews have migrated away from Jewish community to seek spiritual nourishment in other traditions, is certainly not missed by those concerned with Jewish continuity.

As my interviews went on, I became particularly intrigued by individuals who, despite their pain, had found the inner means to stop and ask themselves difficult questions about their lives and the larger context of their injuries. Questions like: *Who am I now? What social and political conditions shaped my tragedy? What can I do to prevent this kind of suffering for others? What meaning can I make of this?*

This kind of critical inquiry was a principal factor among those who found a sense of freedom from the consequences of their injuries. Simply asking questions is a statement of personal agency. On this topic, Frankl turns to Nietzsche's words: "The survivor who knows the 'why' for his existence, will be able to bear almost any 'how.'"[7]

The Principles

Seven distinct themes emerged from my interviews with survivors. Each of them had made a journey through some of the darkest territory a human soul can travel, where, at least for a time, they had no sign of direction, purpose, or hope. Those who stood out for me shared a powerful determination to wrestle with the dark angels that their traumas had brought into their lives: the rage, shame, alienation, hatred of self and other.

I began to notice certain commonalities in the ways these individuals had made it through (rather than around) their respective hells. Many of them had, over long periods of time, lost hope, closed down, surrendered to inertia. But they ultimately reclaimed their sense of self and their place in the world. I am wildly suspicious of reductive formulas, and surely, when dealing with catastrophic events and their traumatic aftermaths, it would be foolish to look for a series of "steps to healing." Every survivor's journey is *sui generis*. Moreover, as many trauma-informed therapists and doctors have attested, the process of trauma integration does not move in a straightforward manner. There is no simple blueprint for recovery.

Nevertheless, my stacks of trauma testimonies revealed shared themes, common denominators that point in distinct directions. I came to see them as principles of Jewish cultural healing. I worked with them, questioned, and tested them. And I now believe these principles are fundamental to both personal and collective Jewish healing.

Shattered Yet Whole

Before sharing the seven principles, a brief story—a crystal, if you will—that shone for me with exceptional light.

Reuven is a robust Romanian Jew with a full head of gray hair. Our first meeting was in the empty lobby of his high-rise Jerusalem apartment.

Born in 1928, Reuven was a refugee from the age of twelve to nineteen, constantly on the move through Central Europe with seven other members of his family. During that time, they endured a dozen expulsions under Antonescu, the Iron

Guard, the Nazis, and the Red Army, often foraging for food, sleeping outside, or giving thanks for whatever hovel was available.

Oddly, as Reuven enumerated his family's extreme privations, his tone was flat. He spoke with a rote quality, as if it was someone else's story.

Then about thirty minutes into our interview, Reuven's eyebrows lifted and a mischievous spark flashed in his gray eyes. "Would you like to hear something?" he asked. "Of course!" I answered.

Looking around the apartment lobby, content that no one else was there, he slid a harmonica out of his breast pocket and began to play a beautiful, mournful tune. I closed my eyes and listened to the haunting melody as it reverberated against the stucco walls. When I opened my eyes, Reuven was smiling broadly. He winked at me, his face now shining, and put his instrument away.

"It was seven years even before we were first expelled," he told me. "Something special happened then. On the wall of our little village pub, I found a violin left from the Gypsies[8]; they must have been very drunk. Like us [Jews], they were always being chased, and no one came back for it. I took it down from the wall and I was very surprised I could play [by ear.] The first song I ever played was 'Hatikva,' the Israeli anthem, 'The Hope'. I knew [it] because my older brother organized a group of youngsters, Zionists, and it was like a *schlager*, a famous song.

"No one could understand how each melody they asked me to play I played. I had perfect pitch then. When we were expelled, my mother prohibited me from taking this violin, but I took it anyway and hid it. Then my little brother sat on it and broke it; I think there were about fifty [broken] parts. A gypsy succeeded in gluing it together. I took it with me everywhere we went and it became my *parnasa* [livelihood]."

After a homeless childhood, Reuven finally arrived in Palestine in 1947 and became a member of the Zionist Socialist youth movement, *Dror haBonim*. He was briefly sent back to Europe to recruit other young fighters for Israel's 1948 War of Independence. He has remained in Israel ever since.

"Do you still play the violin?" I asked Reuven.

"Yes, I have a very old violin," Reuven answered with a proud nod. "The first thing I did when I arrived here and [the government] gave me ten pounds. I went to a market, and the moment I saw a violin, I gave them the ten pounds."

Months later, when I returned to this story, I saw it in a new light. I realized that Reuven's violin was more than an instrument and the melody he shared with me was more than a pleasantry. This proud octogenarian was telling me something about himself that he could not put into plain words. He had smuggled his fragile handmade treasure throughout Central Europe as a refugee. Like him, the violin had born the forces of war, expulsion, and poverty. Like him, it had been broken to bits—but never irreparably. Reuven was telling me about his own resilience, that he had mysteriously been made whole again, able to light up the room with the music of hope.

PRINCIPLE ONE

Facing the Loss

*"At first I did everything I could to look away. I blamed, I bawled,
I tried to bargain for my life back. One day I finally got it. I realized I
better start facing the mess I'm in 'cause it's not going away.
In fact, it's the only show in town."*
—Melanie

OF ALL THE SURVIVORS OF trauma and catastrophic loss I have encountered, the ones who were ultimately able to heal and move forward in their lives were those who faced their situation directly. Recognizing that we have taken a blow is the first step.

Sometimes we are forced into confronting the "mess" of a traumatic situation—when we are immobilized physically or emotionally, or when life as we have known it has been halted, as in a climatic disaster or bombing. At such times, when life is suddenly unrecognizable, we are literally stopped in our tracks and there is nothing to do but face our new reality.

And then there are the situations when survivors simply cannot remember any part of their injury. We saw this with Kelly, the girl who was overwhelmed by the bullying of her half-brother, and mentally removed herself into a second reality. It was not until Kelly was nineteen that she came to remember what had happened to her.

But what about when events befall us, perhaps just as violently, but leave tracks that are subtler to see? Some traumas allow us to get back on our feet and fake it, at least for a while. I have met many people who have kept going through the motions of life, acting *as if* they were all right, for weeks and even months. But as we have already seen in the Part I stories of Lena, Avi, and Esti, avoiding trauma compounds the havoc, ultimately prolonging the work of healing.

Of course there are the very real demands that come with our immediate crisis. We may have children to feed and get to school, family responsibilities to attend to, and people around us who seem more urgently in need of care than we do. Important functions may keep us going, help us put one foot in front of another, and even generate purpose and meaning. But at some point, we will need to turn and face what has happened.

That turning to face our losses takes courage and fortitude. It may be our greatest act of will to simply face our pain, to go against all the voices that would have us *just keep going*. Tending trauma takes immense patience and inward focus, and enough self-love to allow ourselves time and attention.

Meanwhile, the world grows impatient. It wants us back in the fray, looking good, being productive, getting over it. Our culture lauds us for bucking up and getting back to work. It pressures us to show up with optimism and a smile. Withdrawing from life, we discover, does not win us points, even after catastrophe has hit. In fact, taking time to truly experience our emotions (not to mention showing them), we may risk being judged as maladjusted or even incompetent.

Stopping our lives long enough to face our losses requires going against the current of the culture around us, and this can be extremely difficult to do. One must overcome well-intended social pressures to *get on with life* or *get back in the flow*. It also means discovering (and trusting) our own internal pacing.

I recall how important this was to Daniela, whose journey I discussed in Chapter Four. When the news came that her son Tom had been killed, Daniela was working in a kibbutz hotel, booking and organizing tours. "Very stressful work," she told me. "I would get calls at two or three o'clock in the morning! But sometime during *shiva* I decided: *Unlike my husband, I'm not going back to work. No way can I go back into this pressure!* It was clear.

"Now, looking back, it was the smartest thing I ever did. I didn't want to do anything. So I just stayed home...It was a feeling, not something I decided. I said: *This is what I can do now. This is what I want to do now. This is what is right for me now.* Something in me knew that [the pain] won't go away until I own it fully."

—— *Recognizing That We Are Not Okay* ——

Meeting our pain is a formidable challenge for most people, and it is natural to resist it. I knew one family whose twenty-year-old daughter had been kidnapped and molested in a foreign country. After finally getting her back home safely, the parents could not stop. There were legal proceedings, endless medical tests, and fruitless efforts to find their daughter's abductors. All of these were necessary, up to a point. But then it was time to simply hold this girl and feel the pain of what had happened. The family needed to cry, wail, comfort, embrace, and mourn the innocence that had been lost.

Facing our losses means being willing to look at the new territory of our lives, confront the wreckage, and grieve for what is no longer. It also means experiencing our pain, which may fluctuate from day to day or even hour to hour, and wear a myriad of ugly faces: rage, terror, despair, panic, hatred, futility, feeling run over by a truck, and more.

It is not uncommon to feel emotional whiplash. One day we feel utterly vulnerable, firmly in the grips of grief. The next we see something on the street that triggers an eruption of red-hot rage. Later, we may awaken from a nap immobilized by fear or inertia. The ground keeps shifting underneath us.

We may want to short-circuit our feelings. We may want to medicate our pain away. But ultimately there are no shortcuts to the work of tending our pain. It is a river we must ride, and only when we give in to its unique current do we "arrive" at our destination, meaning, the next stage of our healing process. And although we may need the company and care of others, the impulse to avoid public events, stay to oneself, and reflect inwardly must be honored, at least for a time. At first, decreased stimulation and input from others may allow us to feel the full spectrum and complexity of our emotions.

Among those I worked with, people who resisted the "urge to do" or the admonitions of friends "to pick up and get on with life" were able to better ride the uncharitable waves of their ordeal. For each person, this took as long as they needed. Gradually, their dark hell began to break open and yield some new form of meaning, insight, or awareness. Notably, this new sensitivity came into focus of its own accord, not by willing it.

─────── *When Trauma Looks Normal* ───────

But what about those who genuinely do not know they are suffering? This was the case of Sheldon, an organizational consultant in his sixties. Sheldon was born in a displaced persons camp in Heidenheim, Germany, in 1948. Both of his parents were raised in Tomaszow, a town in Poland that the Nazis evacuated in 1942 to Treblinka, the closest Nazi death camp. Forty-three members of their family perished there. His parents narrowly survived, but were deeply scarred.

Sheldon came to the United States at fifteen months old. He and his sister grew up in close quarters with their parents in a tiny apartment in Brooklyn. Many of the people in their neighborhood were Holocaust survivors. Each of them had experienced their own version of hell.

Unwittingly, Sheldon absorbed his parents' terror, shock, and rage. "I was like a walking Energizer battery, on all the time," he told me. "I didn't understand the currents running through me. I was acting out all over the place; almost destroyed my college career. Unbelievable rage!

"The first time I started to wake up to what I was carrying inside of me was when I was twenty. I remember I went out on a date with this girl named Carol. She was the first woman I knew who had a different lens on life. She started to reflect back what she was feeling from me.

"We were on the subway, and she looked at me and said: 'You really need to get some...you know, help. There is so much oozing out of you that you are not even aware of.' That was the moment when I realized I was off. You know, I had been living in it, I was immersed in it, like in a marinade. So that kind of started my journey."

After graduate school, Sheldon and his girlfriend followed a meditation teacher named Rudi and left New York.

"I ran from my roots and the pressure. The pressure had to do with being the firstborn male in a family that had survived. I was *the hope*. I was going to carry the family name. Anyway, we picked up and moved to an ashram.

"Why? Because I found something and someone who actually tried to make sense out of life. Rudi taught us to break down, synthesize, and absorb what you are feeling—into some energy you can actually deal with. [The ashram] felt like an oasis. We were there for seven years."

Unlike my brother Danny, whose move to a Zen monastery proved to be isolating, Sheldon's relocation to an ashram in the mountains of Colorado launched him into a new life. Within the safe container provided by an intentional spiritual community and structured lifestyle, Sheldon learned to tame his mind and face into the intergenerational legacy he was carrying.

———— *The Normalization of Trauma* ————

Whether we call it dissociation, emotional numbing, or psychological splitting, the complete absence from ourselves after trauma can be difficult to detect because our body and brain have united to protect us from feeling the overwhelming pain of our circumstances. Loving friends can give us clues, like Carol did for Sheldon. But what happens when everyone around us is also suffering the effects of the same or similar trauma?

When trauma becomes "normal," how do we begin to recognize that we are not okay?

Recently, I received a call from Katia, a twenty-nine-year-old woman who grew up in Sderot, Israel, and came to the United States to work and study. Katia and her extended family had immigrated to Israel from the Soviet Union when she was three years old, due to religious persecution there.

At our first meeting Katia told me she needed help unlocking the stored trauma she holds in her body. "What makes you think you have stored trauma?" I asked her. "My life is not full," she replied. "I sense it when I hear friends tell painful stories from their lives. I have a cognitive appreciation for their pain, but no feeling. I know there's more."

I asked Katia to tell me about growing up in a place that is called the "Bomb Shelter Capital of the World." She replied: "In Sderot, bombs are falling all the time. Sometimes thirty times a day. Kassam rockets are homemade missiles, blindly shot over the border from Gaza. Most of them fall in the fields, but not all. Our roads are full of deep holes. You get used to it. You learn to drive around them."

Located less than a mile from the Palestinian territory of Gaza, Sderot has been the target of ongoing rocket attacks launched by Hamas and the Palestinian Islamic Jihad since 2001. Although casualties from these rockets have been relatively minimal,[1] their main result is psychological trauma and disruption of daily life in Israeli populations centers. According to one study carried out in 2007,[2] roughly seventy-five percent of Sderot's population suffered from PTSD at the time. And the cycle of violence has only continued.[3]

"Now every building and house by code must have a built-in bomb shelter connected to it. But growing up, it wasn't like that," Katia continued. "You'd hear a woman's voice come over the loud speaker announcing: *Tzeva Adom! Code Red!* And everyone would drop what they were doing and run to the shelter. You get fifteen seconds to run and hide.

"We were sitting together [in the bomb shelter] but there was no talking, no togetherness. No one looks at anyone else. You keep your head down. Everyone just waits and listens. Sometimes you hear the rocket whistle through the air. You wait for the explosion, and as soon as you hear it, like clockwork, everyone picks up and gets on their way. Without speaking, or connecting, or registering any expression at all."

Dodging Missiles

"As a child, I didn't recognize how traumatic this was. We would say: *People from Sderot are Warriors!* And when we heard [Israeli] planes over Gaza bombing them, it makes you feel: *See? We are stronger!*

"But that kind of relief is mental. Whenever I would hear [the bombs] or see the mushroom clouds rise from our strikes, I'd have a twisting in my stomach. I'd know in my core that this is not okay. These things are locked in my body. I couldn't express it to anyone that this is not okay."

I asked Katia about her earliest memories. "I have almost no memories from before the age of eight," Katia told me. "Only what I have pieced together from pictures and stories."

Lack of memory for an entire segment of life is a common symptom of extreme or prolonged trauma. As we have seen, the mind can block out large swathes of memory that it cannot process, and sometimes this means entire segments of life. As was the case for Katia, this can produce frustration and a sense of disconnection from oneself.

"It was only when I moved [to the U.S.] after army service that I started noticing how cynical I was. I had this bitterness in me. For instance, when Americans would tell stories about their growing up, I would say to myself: *Oh, so while I was dodging missiles you were getting ready for the prom!* I began to see how judgmental I was.

"[Another] thing that made me realize how 'ginormous' [my trauma] is was how many times growing up during the [Second] Intifada I had to clutch and hold my breath. About twice every week, buses or restaurants were exploding. You would open the TV and hear the words: *Pigua!* Terror attack!

"But if the people hit were not 'yours,' someone you knew, you were thankful, but that was the entire range of emotion. *Ein mah l'hitloneyn!* is the expression. *Nothing to complain about!* Move on!

"During the Intifada, on the radio they would announce the names of those hit. You would listen and clutch. If you didn't know anyone, [you could] release. Everyday the front page of the newspaper would be covered with, say, thirty-five faces of people who had died in yesterday's terror attack. You know, like small passport photos. My eyes would scan quickly down the page, looking: *Do I know anyone here? No? Shew! I'm okay.* Then you move on."

I asked Katia if there are services in Israel for the kind of stress she was describing. "Yes, of course," she answered with a quizzical look, "but who am *I* to take up time about *my* trauma? I would be [considered] a traitor to even talk about this. We were told: 'Our parents and grandparents fought these wars, and if we don't continue to do that we won't have a country.'

"To admit fear? No way. There's something un-Israeli about that. PTSD is allowed to combat soldiers only, people on the front lines. Unless you've suffered like that, you keep going."

When she arrived to Colorado to begin university studies, Katia chose to live in a big house with other Israeli students. Together, they face their high-intensity backgrounds around the dinner table and in their celebrations of Shabbat and other Jewish rituals. They discuss what it means to have grown up in Israel and unravel what Katia calls their *netunim*, the "givens" or assumptions that come with being raised in a culture that finds itself ceaselessly at war or under threat.

For Katia, being in a safe and loving environment at a considerable remove from her home of origin gave her the emotional safety she needed to face her past and begin doing her healing work. She understood that her past experiences translated directly into physically stored memories. With the help of regular EMDR sessions, Katia began to access these memories, layer by layer. She also received acupuncture for the physical pain that seemed to be the body component of the psychological stress she had stored away.

These body-centered therapy sessions not only helped Katia retrieve her traumatic memories, but also shifted the associated patterns that were keeping her feeling stuck. For example, she discovered that intertwined with her memories of sitting in the bomb shelter as a girl were the intense feelings of aloneness for being a Russian in the largely Moroccan population of Sderot. She remembered her old sadness about her family's dull poverty and a belief that she had no innate richness or color to share. Working with these issues of self-worth and personal responsibility gave Katia an enormous sense of freedom.

Facing our losses requires courage, sensitivity to our internal readiness, and support from others. Katia found all of these resources. The work of integrating her Jewish cultural trauma continues. With a hand on her chest, Katia confided in me, "The presence of my community helps me to do this— to be in my heart and look at all my blind spots."

PRINCIPLE TWO

Harnessing the Power of Pain

"We have an enormous ally on our side: the power of pain.
It is very much like nuclear energy. You can use this energy in order
to bring darkness and destruction and pain, or you can use this
energy to bring light and warmth and hope."
—Rami Elhanan

TRAUMA DISCONNECTS US FROM OUR bodies. Once we have turned to face our situation, we must learn to reinhabit our physical selves. By reclaiming our bodies, we can begin to harness the overwhelming intensity of our experience and put it to use.

In Chapter Two, we saw how the shock of overwhelming events disturbs the balance between the sympathetic nervous system (which arouses us to danger and calls the body and brain to action) and the parasympathetic nervous system (which helps us rest, digest, and heal).

To cope with the hyperarousal that can result from traumatic experience, some may take refuge in numbing activities like television, video games, sleeping, or overeating, which serve to dull our minds and bodies from the endless replay of memories activated by trauma. Or we may take to more sensation-seeking behaviors to compensate for the intensity of our pain, like gambling, heightened sexual activity, or aggressive behaviors like cutting ourselves, or fighting with others.

Our society's modes of coping often contribute to the problem. Many doctors still rely heavily on medications to help their patients alleviate the intensity of post-traumatic symptoms. Antidepressants such as Prozac, Zoloft, and Effexor, commonly used for depression and anxiety, are often prescribed and may indeed be helpful in the short run, to blunt the terrifying emotions and sensations that arise after a traumatic loss. But the residual images and sensations remain embedded in the nervous system, reminding people that they are still susceptible at any time to further triggering and that their inner state is still volatile.

All of these responses are attempts to gain a sense of control in a world that has gone unmanageably awry. Whether we numb or heighten our sensations, we risk losing connection with what is going on inside our bodies. And it is our body awareness that is the bedrock of our ability to become our own witness so that we can guide ourselves more effectively in the world.

What we are talking about here is getting back the inner feeling that we are in charge of our own lives. Many people call this inner feeling *agency*—knowing you have at least some ability to shape your circumstances. As Dr. Van der Kolk puts it: "Knowing *what* we feel is the first step to knowing *why* we feel that way. If we are aware of the constant changes in our inner and outer environment, we can mobilize to manage them."[1]

Body awareness is critical to reclaiming our lives.

I think of Orna, whom I interviewed several years after she lost her only child in a suicide bombing in Tel Aviv. Badly shaken, Orna withdrew from life. After several months of sequestering herself in her apartment, she began to experience disturbing sensations in her chest, a heart arrhythmia that frightened her.

"Sometimes it felt like my heart was turning somersaults and sometimes like it would burst out of my chest. At that time, I was so isolated, I didn't even know who to call. I finally went to the doctor. That's when I got serious about doing something for myself."

Taking action for Orna meant following her doctor's orders to put away the wine, with which she had been medicating herself, and start moving her body. She enrolled in a restorative yoga class.

"I had to force myself to go at first," Orna told me. "I had cut off my body entirely; it was too full of pain from losing [Aviva], too full of memories of carrying her as a baby, laughing with her, feeling her arms around me. I was a single mother, you know. We were like twins."

——————— *Softening the Armor* ———————

Orna resisted her inertia and stayed with the yoga class. Fortunately, her teacher was trauma-informed, and kept her classes simple and slow: a gentle sequence of breathing and stretching, with calming meditation at the end. In therapeutic yoga, the emphasis is not on executing the postures correctly, but on gradually reinhabiting the body. This is done by bringing breath to areas that have become tight or frozen, paying close attention to what's going on inside, and accepting whatever arises with compassion.

With each yoga session, the gentle rhythm between tension (reaching, stretching, contracting) and relaxation (exhaling, letting go, becoming limp) slowly uncoiled Orna's protective facade and her muscle memory of shock, bracing, and helplessness. She told me that hot tears would flow and her entire body would shake as she lay on the floor at the end of the class. Sometimes she would sob aloud and her teacher would come and hold her until the waves of grief had passed.

"During those sessions, I think I was learning all over again how to breathe," Orna told me. Then she added, "Actually I don't think I ever knew how, or let myself. Even before [losing] Aviva."

Long before her twenty-two-year-old daughter died, Orna was carrying a history of trauma. She was born to parents who had both suffered harrowing escapes from Europe. Orna's mother Bella had escaped the Minsk Ghetto before it was liquidated in the autumn of 1943, leaving behind her parents and four siblings, who later perished in the Sobibor extermination camp.

Narrowly surviving the war in hiding, Bella, still a teen, found herself alone in a displaced person camp in Germany. During the post-war period, Jewish organizations were busy organizing an underground network known as *Brichah*

(Hebrew for flight), which moved thousands of Jews from the DP camps to ports along the Mediterranean Sea. From there, they boarded ships for Palestine. In the summer of 1947, Bella was transported by train to southern France, where she joined 4,500 other Jewish refugees on board the S.S. Exodus.

But the British, alarmed by the influx of refugees into Palestine, had placed restrictions on Jewish immigration, and forcefully intercepted the Exodus. Bella was rerouted to an internment camp in Cyprus, where she lived for several months in an overcrowded camp with poor sanitation and shortages of clean water.

It was there that Bella met Shmuel, a Hungarian Jew who had already been interned in Cyprus for two years. Beleaguered and emotionally unsteady from the turbulence of war and their respective losses, they married in the camp within weeks of knowing each other. The following year, August 1948, they were allowed into the newly formed state of Israel. Orna was their first child, born in 1950.

Orna grew up in a home filled with effusive mother-love, stories of a lost world, and fearful parents who kept a tight watch over her. As an heir to her parents' trauma legacy, Orna knew all about managing pain through a strategy of armoring herself against life's blows. Like many Israelis, Orna wears a formidable, no-nonsense exterior. It was on our second meeting that she began to reveal a more tender side.

"I have always had a strong façade," Orna told me, "but behind it there are many other things. I have a sort of tendency to be depressed, and in spite of what you may think, because I am outwardly friendly, I tend to see the negative side of life, of people. But I'm working on myself now."

Along with Orna's yoga classes, I was interested to hear that she had begun to attend Overeaters Anonymous in Tel Aviv. I asked her if food had become a problem since Aviva was killed.

"No," she replied. "This is part of my Holocaust heritage: that the value of food is equal to life itself. My mother was so irrational about food and about my health. She was always in a panic that I [would] not grow and I [would] not be healthy, so she kept feeding me."

Orna was gaining many new skills that helped her inhabit her body and experience more agency in her daily life. The practice of trauma-informed yoga and breathing twice weekly helped her body to release layers of emotional pain that had been frozen in her muscles and core for decades. As her physical armor softened, so did her judgments of herself and others.

In addition, meditating increased Orna's inner focus and awareness of subtle physical sensations and cues. Scientists call this *interoception*—a kind of inner witness that comes from increased body awareness.[2] Finally, Orna stopped medicating herself with excessive alcohol and food consumption. This helped her to clear her mind and feel more alive.

The ability to ground the aftershocks of the traumatic blast that has occurred in our lives, regain a sense safety in our bodies, and befriend rather than suppress the energies that are released by our inner experience are all critical steps to moving forward in the healing journey.

—— *Hair-Triggered and Ready for a Fight* ——

As we have said, the integration and transformation of trauma is a long-term process, one that requires real commitment and abundant self-compassion. But what happens when we do not undertake the work, but rather continue to numb our awareness or suppress our visceral signals by overriding them?

When we are not attuned to our bodies and do not notice what is going on inside of ourselves, we are more vulnerable to being reactive to the many outward and inner triggers that arise each day. Fear, panic, and reactivity are natural reflexes when our trauma has not yet been integrated. Our sympathetic nervous system remains on high alert, just waiting for the next alarm to go off. We live in an anticipatory world, vigilant for any sign of threat, real or imagined, sometimes lashing out disproportionately to what is warranted by our outward situation.

As I discussed in Chapter Two, it is not uncommon to become physiologically hooked on this kind of activation, organizing oneself around the theme of defense, constantly on the lookout for trouble. We have all known or heard of soldiers or first-responders who return from the field of duty with hair-trigger temperaments. Such hyperarousal obviously interferes with making rational choices, and sets the stage for further injury, either to ourselves or to others.

———————— *Still We Are Haunted* ————————

Although neuroscience has taught us a lot about how individuals react to traumatic experiences, we are still in the early stages of awareness about the long-term effects of collective social violence. We have yet to fully understand, for example, how ongoing oppression or atrocities committed on an entire nation or ethnic group shape the group's evolving collective psychology. But we can certainly take some clues from the responses of our neighbors.

The African American community—whose collective trauma, like that of the Jews—is still active, has endured hundreds of years of dehumanization and oppression in the United States. Today, on the other side of official institutional slavery, the remnants of African Americans' centuries of oppression are still visible in the racial discrimination, economic suppression, and daily street brutality that many black people suffer in America.

For many years, the black community regulated their responses to ongoing structural and social injustices in America, in an effort to gain the respect and recognition of the dominant culture. Then there was an explosion, and collective trauma boiled to the surface. Black writers from James Baldwin to Malcolm X began naming the depths of systemic oppression, documenting discriminatory housing segregation, police persecution, and the denial of opportunities for wealth accrual.

Why are black people so upset? whites asked. *Wasn't slavery long gone? Isn't segregation illegal now? Blacks can vote, get educated, even run for office nowadays.* It was all too easy to look away from the ongoing injustices and the legacy of trauma—one that afflicted both victim and perpetrator.

"Now we have half-stepped away from our long centuries of despoilment, promising, 'Never again.' But still we are haunted," writes journalist and educator Ta-Nehisi Coates. "It is as though we have run up a credit-card bill and, having pledged to charge no more, remain befuddled that the balance does not disappear. The effects of that balance, interest accruing daily, are all around us."[3]

Indeed, watching replays of riots and demonstrations, from Watts in 1965 to Ferguson in 2014, one senses the historical trauma of the African American community swelling just below the surface, repeatedly rising to a boiling-point over "one more" racially motivated killing, one more bogus traffic arrest, one more brutal death at the hands of white police. "Two hundred fifty years of slavery. Ninety years of Jim Crow. Sixty years of separate but equal. Thirty-five years of racist housing policy," writes Coates. "Until we reckon with our compounding moral debts, America will never be whole."[4]

Unlike blacks, Jews have enjoyed considerable entry into American institutions in the last several decades. At least outwardly, Jews have begun to outgrow the degrading stereotypes and exclusionary bans that white America placed upon them. But the privileges Jews have taken for granted—education, social and political power, wealth accumulation, to name a few—have been, some say, provisionally conferred upon them by their mostly light-colored skin, which has made it easier to blend into American society.

Nevertheless, Jews and African Americans share a history of traumatic persecution. These commonalities have historically engendered a natural affinity, one that was most apparent in the early days of the Civil Rights Movement, when hundreds of Jewish civil rights workers, legal aids activists, and Freedom Riders flocked to the southern United States to advocate for African American equality. In that period many Jews made great sacrifices to assist in the black struggles, in some way connected to the moral imperatives that came with Jewish prophetic values. As one Freedom Rider friend explained to me about that era, it was simply "what you did if you were Jewish."

Now, in the twenty-first century, as racial and ethnic bigotry rears its ugly head once again, the legacy of historical trauma is being activated in the Jewish community as in the African American community. It roils the blood of Jews around the world to watch neo-Nazis march in the streets with torches held high, yelling, *Jews will not replace us!* as they did in Charlottesville in the summer of 2017. And just so, it must arouse the cellular memory of African Americans to watch the gunning down of innocent black men, women, and even children on streets all over America by uniformed police officers. In both cases, the collective body screams: *Never again!*

Limbic Lava

It was the summer of 2006, just after war had broken out between Israel and Lebanon. Hezbollah had fired rockets at Israeli border towns leaving three Israeli soldiers dead and two abducted. It looked as though these events might escalate into another full-scale war with Lebanon,[5] and tensions were running high in Jewish communities around the world.

A prayer vigil was called at the largest synagogue in town, and many public officials were invited to attend. The sanctuary was packed on that hot July night, and the crowd was grave. I was seated with other rabbis on the dais that July evening, along with city council members, state senators, and even a US representative to Congress.

Prayers and words of encouragement were delivered. Then, halfway through the program, a young government official closed his otherwise supportive address with the hopes that all sides, including Israel, "would act with self-restraint."

Instantly, a fury broke out. What had been only seconds earlier a stiffly prayerful audience suddenly turned bellicose. Brows furrowed, both men and women began hissing and booing loudly. A few individuals rose to their feet, indignantly striking their fists in the air. Curiously, there were no words used, only primal sounds and gestures. Finally, others in the audience shushed the noisy outbreak.

The unwitting official had naively tripped over an invisible redline, activated when his Jewish audience registered a dangerous threat implicit in his words. Perhaps they had heard what they feared most: that Israel must not defend herself against a murderous enemy, but remain passive to the aggression of her neighbors without recourse. This was the hair-trigger: Jews had been passive in the Holocaust. Never again would they be sheep led to slaughter!

Self-defense is an unquestionable right, for Israel and for any person or group that is under life-threatening attack. Many Jews still carry the collective memory of their genocide at a visceral level. The point here is that hyperarousal can show up in any group that carries a history of near annihilation, and much like it does in individuals, it activates the limbic response of an entire group, that segment of the human nervous system that is responsible for survival at all costs. When that happens, what might be figuratively called *limbic lava* flows, and reasoned, well-considered responses are rarely made.

—— *Interrupting the Cycle of Trauma* ——

From this vantage point, it is easy to understand how unprocessed trauma is repeated and perpetuated. Once the triggering cycle has been set into motion, and the more judicious cortical brain is offline, the fight-flight-freeze reaction takes over. Whether we are talking about an individual or an entire nation, the physiological compulsion to react fogs the rational mind. Then our survival instinct takes over, just as it did for the dignified Jews in the synagogue that evening. We shoot from the hip, fire off missives that offend, or missiles that destroy, and the cycle of damage continues.

This creates a tragic dilemma for survivors of trauma. As Bessel van der Kolk puts it: "Many traumatized people expose themselves, seemingly compulsively, to situations reminiscent of the original trauma. These behavioral reenactments are rarely consciously understood to be related to earlier life experiences."[6] Abuse victims tend to attract abusive situations, veterans of war redeploy, and entire ethnic groups can find themselves again and again under attack, fighting back endlessly.

How can we stop the cycle? Again, this requires a strong interior container made of sound body and mind, one that can tolerate and temper the injustice and mortal affront that we have endured. As we become aware of our pain and harness the intensity we hold inside, we are no longer compelled to replay the same script.

―――― *Channeling the Nuclear Power* ――――

"This is a wound that never heals," Rami told me, speaking of the loss of his fourteen-year-old daughter in a Jerusalem suicide bombing. "Out of every sixty seconds, out of every day, it's there. If people tell you that time heals, it's completely untrue. I am always amazed by the 'irresistible easiness of continued living.' But [the pain] is unbearable. How can you go on living as if nothing has ever happened?"

After losing Smadar, Rami became a dark tempest of cynicism and rage; he could easily have perpetrated another cycle of violence. But one specific moment, a turning point, opened him to new awareness. It was the moment he stopped to watch a group of grieving parents descend from a bus. All of them were wounded, Israeli war heroes and Palestinian farmers alike. A Palestinian mother wearing her daughter's picture around her neck had triggered in Rami a quantum leap.

This was Rami's subtle moment of choice. He allowed himself to see the utter humanity of his so-called enemy. "After that, I realized I could not go back to my old way of being."

Rami taught me that extreme pain can be our ally. "It is very much like nuclear energy," he explained. We can use it to bring about more pain, darkness, and destruction. Or we can harness it to bring about light, warmth, and hope. Ultimately, the choice belongs to us.

Soon after his realization, Rami joined the Parent Circle-Families Forum and began speaking out about the conditions that caused the loss of so many children like Smadar.

"I found a reason to get out of bed in the morning: the ability to look into the eyes of Israeli or Palestinian kids before they go into the army or into the 'terrorist organizations.'" (Here, Rami drew air quotes with his fingers.) "To put a crack, some doubt, some question mark into their thinking. And believe me when I say, I see the effect of it. I see one kid at the end of the class nodding his head in acceptance. Every nod of the head is a miracle. And I see so many miracles.

"Of course," Rami added with a sigh, "I have no illusions. It is a long and bumpy road. We are like people who are drawing water from the ocean with a spoon. But I think we are making a difference."

Principle Three

Finding New Community

*"I knew I had to find others with whom I could relate and be myself.
I was different now, and I needed a different approach."*
—Tamara Rabinowitz

"**T**RAUMA IS ABOUT BROKEN connections...with the body/self, family, friends, community, nature, and spirit," writes trauma psychologist Peter Levine. "Healing trauma is about restoring these connections."[1]

As we have seen earlier, ending our isolation—having what I've called a witness to our pain—is a critical ingredient of recovery. But traumatized people often find it difficult to trust that their story will be fully heard and received, and indeed reliable witnesses may be hard to find.

This is especially true when the teller cannot easily be soothed, or when their story uncovers social problems others would prefer to ignore, or when it exposes the dark side of a family, institution, or nation. Then, in the absence of compassionate listeners, a new layer of estrangement sets in, pushing the trauma survivor farther away from belonging.

And yet survivors know instinctively that wholeness lies dormant within their wound, and that an authentic connection with someone who can tolerate their pain may help them heal.

This often means that trauma survivors must find new social networks, for they are different people now, unknowable to their old selves. This process of making new connections may begin with just one person in whom they can confide. If they are fortunate, they will find a group of like-minded people who can understand their suffering because the listeners themselves have been there.

Rejoining the World

Lena, the artist who at age seven lost her cousin in a car accident, came to me when she recognized that the trauma had frozen her in time and derailed her development. When she was a teen, her parents had sent her to boarding school, perhaps because they found her pain too difficult to tolerate, and hoped she might find some friends. But Lena retreated even further into her self-protective cocoon, avoiding sports or any kind of socializing that she deemed to be frivolous. Those years were excruciating for her, and she formed a strong pattern of self-sequestering.

Well after Lena and I had established our therapeutic alliance, she would still retreat into her "zone of silence" when the work got rough. I gradually learned to give her space, to wait for her to come to her own insights in her own time.

About two years into our work together, shortly after Lena began practicing yoga, she heard about a local women's art collective. After several months of wondering if she would qualify, Lena timidly asked if she could join. She was taken aback when the artists welcomed her into their circle and invited her to attend their weekly meetings.

There, they discussed their work and shared how their inner journeys were being expressed through art. Lena found in them an emotionally safe and responsive community, and more—it was also a circle where pragmatic help was available to her. It became a source of networking, news about local exhibits, and even marketing advice, all of which encouraged Lena to take her art to the next level.

A Dilemma for Caregivers

For therapists, pastoral caregivers, and caseworkers, working with traumatized individuals can be extremely demanding. It requires full attention and an ability to stay neutral and responsive to stories that are often heart-wrenching, horrifying, or simply irrational. Especially at the outset of treatment, a professional caregiver may be the client's only authentic connection, a precious but weighty responsibility.

I have found it critical to monitor my own wellbeing while assisting traumatized individuals. As a rabbi, being called to the emergency room in the middle of the night, or to the aftermath of a bad accident, or to the home where a disaster, suicide, or domestic violence has occurred, I have been left with a kind of secondary or vicarious trauma that is hard to shake. This is not uncommon for caregivers.

Sleeplessness, social withdrawal, overwhelming fatigue, or feelings of anger, despair, and anxiety are all signs that it is time to step back and attend to oneself. We caregivers need to do our own intensive psychological work if we are to be truly effective and remain emotionally available. It is all too easy to project our own needs, fears, or judgments onto our clients.

One of the biggest traps for caseworkers, clergy, and therapists dealing with extreme trauma is the belief that we are the only resource—that the client's wellbeing depends entirely upon us. This can lead to a subtle kind of inflation, which can easily flip into isolation, burn-out, and even a kind of paralysis for the caregiver. This is another reason why trauma survivors need more than individual support.

When a client lacks a personal circle of support, I sometimes recommend twelve-step programs, particularly when addictive tendencies are showing up. Just as Orna found help at Overeaters Anonymous when she turned to food for comfort after her daughter was killed, Narcotics Anonymous, Adult Children of Alcoholics, and Emotions Anonymous are safe havens where survivors can share their troubled past without fear of judgment or recrimination. In such groups it becomes clear that we are all part of a larger community, all working to heal in some way.

Reaching Out

Support groups and resource centers that address Jewish historical trauma in its various forms are abundant. Among

Ashkenazi Jews, for whom the Holocaust is the central cata-strophic event of modern Jewish history, survivors and their offspring can find camaraderie in Holocaust survivors' sup-port groups, offered in most cities in North America, Israel, and Europe that have a Jewish community.

Second Generation Holocaust Survivors (2G) groups are increasingly prolific, especially now that the actual survivors are nearing the end of their lives. And Third Generation and Grandchildren of Holocaust Survivors groups (3G) have sprung up in many cities for the next generation of Jewish Holocaust descendants who wish to preserve the legacies of their older relatives, as well as explore how their grandparents' trauma might be influencing their own generation.[2]

I think of Sheldon, who first found refuge from his in-tense post-Holocaust upbringing in a rigorous yoga ashram. In that safe and supportive spiritual community, he learned how to meditate and tame the high-speed reactivity he had learned at home. He also developed compassion for himself and others.

Eventually, Sheldon found his way into a progressive Jewish community where he realized the need to examine more di-rectly his Holocaust legacy and the impact it had on him. He enrolled in a Children of Survivors support group. The meet-ings had no formal agenda other than to provide a safe place in which to share and dialogue about family stories. Yet they were pivotal in Sheldon's life.

I asked him what made the group so beneficial.

"There was an incredible safety there," he told me, "being able to talk about our experiences with people who just *get it*. Even though everyone's history was different.

"But no matter the level of intensity [of our families' suffering], there was a baseline acceptance among us," Sheldon said, "an instantaneous respect for the fact that your family came through such horror, and that you have an important story to tell."

──────── *Differing Jewish Histories* ────────

For descendants of Jews from Central and East Europe, the question *Where was your family during the war?* is immediately understood in terms of the Nazi regime and its atrocities. But the intense focus on the Nazi Holocaust and its legacy does not speak for all Jews. Because most Jews in America are of Ashkenazic descent, it is easy to forget (or be ignorant of) the fact that the Jewish world is far more diverse, both ethnically and racially.

For Sephardic Jews (with ancestral roots in Spain, Portugal, and North Africa) and Mizrahi Jews, who hail from all over the Middle East (including Azerbaijan, Iran, Uzbekistan, the Caucasus, and Pakistan) as well as India, history tells a very different story.

For these Jews, many of whom fled Muslim countries in the 1950s and now represent the majority of Jews in Israel, modern Jewish history centers around a series of very different historical events that unfolded in their part of the world.

Jewish life flowered in many ways under the 600-year reign of the Ottoman Empire. Many Jews achieved intellectual, financial, and political influence; some even wielded power within the dynasty's royal courts. But Jews also suffered through periods of heavy discrimination and religious persecution under the Islamic dynasty.

By the early twentieth century, after decades of European expansion and colonization, culminating in the abolition of the Ottoman caliphate, radical changes came for the Jewish community in Muslim countries. With both Arab and Jewish nationalism burgeoning, anti-Semitism, which had previously been episodic, became oppressive for Jews living in the Middle East.

Many in the Arab world seized on the emergence of the State of Israel in 1948, blaming it for the loss of Arab autonomy.[3] The very existence of the Jewish state, compounded by its military victories against Arab states in 1956 and 1967, unleashed torrents of anti-Semitic decrees, pogroms, and expulsions in the Arab Peninsula and throughout the Muslim world.[4]

Jews who had lived and flourished in Iran for 2,700 years, were increasingly targeted. Over 60,000 Jews left Iran from the 1950s to the early '80s. Especially virulent anti-Jewish sentiment broke out during the revolution of the late 1970s. Seen as the Shah's allies, Jews were suddenly accused of plundering Iran's wealth. Hateful graffiti began appearing on the walls of synagogues and Jewish schools; pamphlets were circulated declaring revenge upon the Jews.

As we saw in the case of Esti and her family, Jews who had been successfully embedded in the Iranian culture were forced to flee, leaving their property and businesses behind.

Another Exodus from Egypt

Timna, an Israeli of Egyptian descent,[5] came to the United States in 2007 after serving in the Israeli army. Wanting to see the world, she found her way to Miami, where she had cousins. Once she established herself there, she enrolled in university. But her family's difficult history, compounded with several traumatic events she encountered while serving in the Israel Defense Forces, weighed upon her.

By the time Timna contacted me, she was a graduate student in Boston. She was seeking help writing a paper about the impact of intergenerational trauma on the Mizrahi Jewish community and the role that community can play in healing.

"I was never so lonely as when I moved to the United States," Timna told me. "In Israel there are Jews from all over the world, but I always had a feeling of community. When I got here, I didn't fit in with other kids on campus, not even the Jewish kids. They assumed I was like them, but I wasn't.

"I consider myself to be a Middle Eastern Jew," Timna told me proudly. "We have our own past to heal from, no less than Ashkenazic Jews, who sometimes have an attitude. You know, it's a kind of moral superiority because of the Holocaust."

Then to her relief, Timna discovered a program on campus sponsored by JIMENA, Jews Indigenous to the Middle East and North Africa.[6] The first meeting she attended featured a speaker from Libya, herself a Jewish refugee, who asked the audience to form small groups and share stories about their families of origin. For the first time, Timna met other students from Sephardi and Mizrahi backgrounds.

"Some were like me, Arab Jews born in Muslim countries. And some were American born, of Mizrahi descent. But it didn't matter; we all shared a bond. We were a minority within a minority, you can say. I was at home in this group. I could tell them anything."

I asked Timna to tell me her family story.

"My mother's parents were expelled from Egypt in 1956, and came to Israel before she was born. My father came over later—as a ten-year-old in 1962—old enough to see some bad stuff and be scared."

Timna's father was born the year Nasser came into power, 1952, and Jewish life in Egypt was becoming dangerous. After the Suez War in 1956, Egyptian Jews were equated with the "imperialist enemy." Timna's grandparents had their bank accounts frozen, and they were forced to sign papers saying they were 'donating' their business and all their property to the state.

"[My sisters and I] were raised with stories about Dad's 'exodus from Egypt,' that's what he called it jokingly. I remember his stories as if I lived through them myself. I still dream about them to this day. How the Egyptian secret police came to his house in the middle of the night and banged on the door. [And how] they barged in, hollering accusations at my grandparents that they were Zionist spies.

"They got them out of their beds and turned the house upside down. They tore mattresses and pillows apart with knives, and smashed furniture, and emptied drawers on the floor. They were searching for weapons, or some kind of proof that my family were spies, traitors to Egypt.

"Of course they weren't. They had it good in Egypt and didn't want to leave. Not that it was great there. The Muslim Brotherhood was already a problem, and there were anti-Zionist demonstrations. A synagogue in Cairo was even burned down. But my grandfather had a good business and they had roots there.

"I have this picture frozen in my mind of my dad and his little sisters huddled in the corner with their mom in their pajamas," Timna added. "I think he still has PTSD from that night. Maybe I do, too. But just knowing that an organization like JIMENA is out there to support people like me gives me feelings of pride."

——————— *Alone, I Felt Crazy* ———————

The Israeli veterans I interviewed also had a complex need for connection. Their army experiences had revealed to them what might be called the underbelly of certain military operations and policies in their country. They had been traumatized by what they had seen and what they had themselves done, yet many kept silent, fearing that their inner conflicts would upset friends, family, and military superiors.

"Alone, I felt crazy," one IDF veteran I will call Sammy told me. "I had piled up too much inside, with nowhere to put it. These were things that needed to be talked about, but you couldn't say them out loud."

Sammy has black curly hair and big dark eyes, revealing his Iraqi Jewish heritage. "On my father's side, we have been in Jerusalem for ten generations," he told me proudly. "My mother's people are Hungarian. They came to Israel just after the war."

I asked Sammy to tell me about the experiences that changed him.

"Okay," he agreed. "But before I tell you what happened on duty, let me say something about my childhood. My first memories are of waking up in the middle of the night to my grandmother's screams. She often screamed at night and woke us all up. It was terrifying. She had been in Auschwitz and never got over it.

"Whenever this happened, my mother would rush into our room to comfort me and my siblings. She explained to us that Grandma was having bad dreams about the war again, and that she couldn't help it. I would ask my mother: *But why do they hate us? Why do they want to kill us?*

"When I went into the army, I got training for intense war. But I had no preparation for what I would experience in Hebron: 180,000 Palestinians, with Jews at the center controlling it all. But somehow I liked the power. I was like an action hero, I'm ashamed to say it now.

"One night I was awakened at four o'clock in the morning by a buddy who had the night watch. He had this crazed look in his eyes. *I think we just killed a little boy,* he was saying over and over. Just then, the alarm goes off and we get called up on a mission, into the Arab quarter. We get on our vests and grenades, the works.

"I suddenly realized we were being brought outside the home of the little boy that was shot. A drama was happening. The kid had been out after curfew and the soldiers shot him. The family wanted to bury their son, but because of the strict curfew, no Palestinians were allowed out of their houses.

"The father was crazy with grief. He just lost his little boy. *Hallas! Enough of this!* He ran out of his house in protest, and charged the sergeant. The guy was instantly handcuffed and thrown into the jeep.

"Then the mother looked out and saw what was happening. First she loses her little boy and now her husband. And she starts screaming and screaming.

"Those screams of hers in the middle of the night made me shake. It was my grandmother—I mean, it was just like my grandmother in the middle of the night when I was a kid. The same screams! I felt very afraid."

Sammy's turning point occurred that night, when his own childhood trauma was retriggered. Many more realizations followed for him in the following days and in the course of his army duty. He understood viscerally that undigested fear and trauma pass from generation to generation, and even from one nation to another.

When Sammy went home that weekend, he received congratulations from his father, a military man, who had heard of the incident. "Good work! Your guys managed to kill a terrorist!" his father said proudly.

Sammy knew that he had it all wrong, that the story had been skewed, that it was a nine-year-old child who had been shot by mistake. But he said nothing. "I shut down," Sammy said. "But from that point on, something inside me knew I had to change...I didn't recognize myself anymore. I was becoming a violent man."

Sammy's angst drove him to find others. Cautiously, he shared his story with one or two trusted friends. Then he found his way to Breaking the Silence, one of the groups of Israeli reservists and veterans that address moral issues such as Sammy's and Avner's, who had told me he suffered from the "trauma of being the bad guy."

Speaking to these IDF veterans, I realized that they carry a unique form of Jewish historical trauma, one that is for them as damaging as the trauma Jews have suffered from anti-Jewish harassment. But Sammy and his friends risk another form of trauma and isolation: being characterized as traitors by other Jews and the Israeli government.

Nevertheless, Israeli men and women veterans and reservists continue to come together to support each other,[7] and to publicize the problems inherent in the occupation through documentary films, photographs, and written testimonies. Finding their way to other likeminded Israelis, they support one another to maintain their moral compass, speak and dialogue openly, and live lives that are in accord with the principles that they understand lie at the core of Jewish heritage and the country they love.

Principle Four

Resisting the Call to Fear, Blame, and Dehumanize

"I saw this for myself in the camps.... The body has its own will,
its own fears, its own desire for revenge. But the soul has eyes
that can be awakened. Then one sees that while hate
goes on and on forever, there is another path.
One can choose."

—Helena, an Auschwitz survivor

"WHEN YOU GROW UP AS *the other*, as many Jews have around the world," Tamara explained, "it's natural that you will do it, too—you will *'other'* others, I don't know a better way to call it," she said with a shrug.

I was interviewing Tamara Rabinowitz, a seventy-three-year-old South African immigrant who had moved to Israel in 1960 with her husband. They settled in the south of Israel and raised three children. Tamara taught English at a high school largely populated with Bedouin kids, where she struggled to raise educational standards, mediate with troubled families, and keep the teens from dropping out. Life was challenging but full.

Then, in 1987, their eldest son, Idor, was killed in a military accident while serving in the IDF. He was twenty years old.

Life stopped. Tamara quit her job. She no longer had the energy to work with angry Bedouin children. She needed time to mourn and to think.

And this brought Tamara into a confrontation with Israeli culture.

"After Idor's death, people were there for us morning, afternoon, and night, quietly cooking and bringing food, sitting with us and listening. If I told you how people looked after us—friends and complete strangers!—you would not be able to imagine it. I don't think we would have survived.

"The Israeli army looks after the parents of this country. They are incredible. They help you, back you, and support you. They support you for the rest of your lives.

"But after the *shiva* and the intense mourning subsided, I began to diverge. I was never into the patriotic ceremonies. But now I fought against what was always part of Israeli society: the adage, *Tov lamut b'ad artzenu. It's good to die for our country.* As a mother, I simply didn't believe that. Nor could I believe that *every Arab is a terrorist.* That they all hate us. You hear that a lot, too.

"Maybe I am a bit of an outsider. I am not a *sabra.* I never did the army. But maybe for that reason I can see things that others don't.

151

"Like with the blacks [in South Africa], I knew it was wrong, the oppression. We had escaped Hitler and his racist armies. We were the hated *other* then. But we lived with a high wall around us. 'Blacks and their problems are not part of who we are,' we were told. But once I got out into the world, I realized, my God, we are living in this ivory tower!"

Then she added, "Here [in Israel] we do the same with the Arabs."

Life Under Siege

When you grow up as the other...you will "other" others. I took Tamara's words to mean that when we distance ourselves from those who are unlike us, when we make them into the faceless objects of our distrust and fear, we are only one step away from denying their humanity. And so the cycle of violence and trauma is set in motion once again.

Just as individuals can go numb with shock and grief, just as stress hormones can create a continual state of alarm in the body, the same can be true for a society, or for an entire people. As I discussed in Chapter Two, unintegrated trauma leaves us in a permanently defensive relationship to life. Our outer world becomes untrustworthy, and we become isolated in our own mental fortress. In a very real sense, the legacy of unhealed trauma is a life under siege.

The four hallmarks of trauma—dissociation, hyperarousal, isolation, and repetition—that affect the individual human body also affect the body politic. Consider **dissociation,** the natural and even lifesaving mechanism by which a person under threat splits off from reality, both emotionally and mentally. In the moment of crisis, this walling-off of awareness may allow us to continue to function. But in the long term, we risk becoming increasingly disconnected from ourselves and others. If we deaden ourselves to our own pain, we will also deaden ourselves to the pain of others.

Hyperarousal is a state of intense activation and vigilance, in which the stress hormones that once helped us respond to life-threatening danger, now remain permanently elevated, reshaping both our physiology and our thought processes. We are easily triggered by any perceived threat. We are reactive rather than reflective. Physiologically, we become programmed to see danger rather than opportunities.

Isolation is the third hallmark of trauma. In the aftermath of overwhelming events, it is natural to pull back from others so that we can dedicate our energy to the work of recovery. But prolonged isolation can perpetuate the sense that we do not need anyone, that no one can understand or help us. Less permeable to new information and the views of others, our traumatic memories become fixed and inflexible. We become more resistant to change, less open to new opportunities for growth.

The final hallmark of trauma is **repetition**: the paradoxical but well-documented tendency of survivors to find or recreate situations reminiscent of their original trauma. The survivors themselves often struggle to identify the source of such uncanny reiterations of behaviors and even historical events. Trauma has blunted their conscious awareness of the magnitude of their own wounds.

Whether survivors recreate their trauma situation to gain comfort, mastery, or resolution, this pattern remains unconscious and so yields little but further pain.

These four trauma characteristics describe an inner landscape that is shared in varying degrees by trauma survivors the world over. It's important to remember that extreme trauma not only reshapes the lives of those who actually live through overwhelming events. It is a train that rumbles through history, depositing its load into the lives of new generations as well.

———————— *The Need to Build Walls* ————————

In the fall of 2009, I attended a lecture in Jerusalem at which the distinguished Israeli statesman Avraham Burg told this story. It occurred during the Second Intifada[1] when Burg was Speaker of the Knesset. He was invited to a prestigious Jewish high school in Tel Aviv to discuss the national crisis with the students there. This was a time when Palestinian terror attacks, fueled by Islamic propaganda, were killing hundreds of innocent Israeli civilians at bus stops, pizza parlors, and malls. Burg's audience was composed of Jewish teens who would, in the next one to three years, be inducted into the Israeli army.

After Burg had finished his remarks, he invited the students to speak their own minds. Several of them argued vehemently in favor of deportations and transfer of the Palestinians to other countries. Others thought that revenge was justifiable, as was any measure, even the killing of innocents, as a deterrent to Jewish bloodshed. The more passionate speakers were applauded loudly by their fellow students.

The principal of the school listened quietly to this discussion from his seat at the back of the room, but he was visibly upset. Finally, he walked to the front of the classroom and said with a trembling voice: "You are not listening to what you are saying! This is how they spoke about *us* sixty and seventy years ago. This is what they did to *us*." The students fell into silence, but it was clear to Burg that they disagreed with their headmaster.

Today, *othering* remains rampant amongst many of Israel's young, reinforced by the very measures taken to defend Israel's citizens from violence.[2]

In response to the onslaught of suicide bombings and terror attacks of the Second Intifada, the Israeli government set out to prevent Palestinian terrorists from slipping across the border by constructing a security fence (also known as the Separation Barrier). Meant to run along or near the Green Line, the pre-1967 boundary between Israel and the West Bank,[3] it would deter Palestinians bent on violence from entering Israel. In effect, the wall would separate the two populations.

Looking out from the hills around Jerusalem today, one can easily spot Israel's security fence snaking across the landscape in the form of a thirty-foot-high concrete wall. In other regions of Israel, the roughly 500-mile barrier is a chain-link fence armed with electronic sensors. In still others, it takes the form of razor wire or round bales of barbed wire. One can see from an aerial view that in many places Israel's barrier does not follow the Green Line as promised, but gouges deeply into ancestral Palestinian lands.

Seen from the road, the dividing wall on the Israeli side is neutrally aesthetic, and even pleasing to the eye in certain places; for instance, on the highway to Ben Gurion Airport, where it creates a peaceful corridor. On the Palestinian side, the wall is crude, adorned with graffiti art and sprawling, spray-painted words and graphics.

Heated controversy has dogged the barrier's construction from its inception. Palestinians claim that it is a land grab, keeps farmers out of their own orchards and fields, divides communities and families, and as one Arab taxi driver told me, "insults us every day." Over the last fifteen years, Israel's high court has demanded numerous modifications be made to the fence's route to keep it from disrupting Palestinian life and property.

Yet Israel's barrier has in fact accomplished its initial purpose: Since the first years of its construction, the number of terror attacks committed by infiltrators into Israel has declined by well over ninety percent, sparing numerous lives.[4]

—————— *Becoming Faceless* ——————

Nevertheless, a dilemma remains. The enforced separation of peoples (especially when one dominates the other) creates a dangerous and unsustainable situation: the impossibility of ever seeing the *others* in their simple humanity. The polarization brought about by two separate and unequal populations sets the stage for further loss of human dignity, and an endless pattern of violent upheavals results.

In this way, traversing to the other side of the wall has been made all but impossible for Israelis who within memory traveled regularly to Bethlehem or Ramallah for an Arab coffee or a plate of *shakshuka*. Today, most Jews never see Palestinian children at play, or men playing backgammon in the sun, or the extreme disparity in living standards that exists behind the barrier.

On the Palestinian side, it is rare to see a Jew who is not in uniform and armed, patrolling the streets on foot or in an armored military vehicle.[5] Jewish settlers who have taken up residence on what Palestinians consider their ancestral lands are visible only from a distance. They live in neatly planned, gated towns with red-roofed houses, malls, and swimming pools, built atop the hills overlooking Palestinian villages. They drive on their own roads, shop in their own markets, have their own laws and court system.

When people no longer have day-to-day interactions, when they do not eat, work, play, mourn, or celebrate together, there is no basis for normal human relations. Every encounter is stiff, every interaction a cause for suspicion and fear. For each population, the other has become faceless, dreaded, unwanted. Hate speech emerges; policies tighten; the cycle intensifies.

I remember a remark of Avner's, the young Israeli reservist whom I mentioned in Principle Three as a member of Breaking the Silence: "For a lot of Israelis, London is closer than Ramallah. Just ask any well-heeled Jerusalemite how many times he has been to London and how many times he has been in Ramallah. They will say, *Ramallah? It's far! It's dangerous!*"

I had a firsthand experience of this cultural polarization while traveling with an international human rights delegation in 2012. Sitting in a car at the Qalandiya checkpoint[6] with British and American colleagues, we waited for the better part of an hour to enter the Palestinian town. As Israeli soldiers processed our papers, I was taken aback by how young they looked.

One female IDF soldier in particular stands out in my memory. She wore a ponytail, but her furrowed brow was fierce. Peering into our car, she asked incredulously, "Why do you want to go inside [this town]? Don't you know they are all terrorists in there?"

It is understandable that after many cycles of harrowing violence, a society would build a formidable buttress against what is understood to be the hostile encroachment of the *other*. But where there are walls, it is far easier to project hate and blame onto a faceless enemy. Then it is only a matter of time before the consequences of dehumanization become manifest—on both sides of the divide.

Resisting Human Nature

After suffering grave blows, people are far more vulnerable to being manipulated by those in power. Following the attacks of September 11, 2001, for example, while still in the throes of post-traumatic shock, Americans went willingly into an aggressive war in Iraq that had little justifiable logic.

Journalist Naomi Klein addressed this point in her bestselling book, *The Shock Doctrine*. "In moments of crisis," Klein writes, "people are willing to hand over a great deal of power to anyone who claims to have a magic cure—whether the crisis is a financial meltdown or...a terrorist attack."[7]

Sammy, the IDF veteran whose family's trauma was awakened one night in the occupied territory, later told me about his high school field trip to Poland. Along with scores of other Jewish sixteen-year-olds, Sammy traveled to Auschwitz to study what had occurred there.[8]

Sponsored and subsidized by Israel's Ministry of Education, tens of thousands of young Israelis—about one-third of the country's Jewish youth—travel to Poland each year to visit the remnants of Jewish ghettos, cemeteries, and death camps, and learn about the death machine that brought an end to Europe's flourishing Jewish culture.

After three days of walking, hearing lectures, and then debriefing their experience at a hotel in Warsaw, Sammy told me, he and his group were shaken and exhausted.

"We were overcome by what we saw," Sammy recounted. "But also proud. The leaders brought along Israeli flags and some of the kids draped themselves in the flags and wore them in the camps to make a statement.

"After a while it struck me that there was also some manipulation going on. You know, there's nothing wrong with traveling to see these things; it's Jewish history. But too often the message is: *Look what the Goyim did to us. Look how we suffered. But we made it. Now we can do anything we want.*"

Tamara, who named "othering" for me, made a similar point during one of our talks. "There is xenophobia emerging in Israel today," she told me, "Whether it is the ultra-Orthodox, whether it is the Arab, or the Russian, whoever it is, there has become an absolute fear of the *other*.

"And I am sick of hearing that it's because of the *Shoah!*"

"Because of the *Shoah?*" I asked, surprised.

"Yes," she answered. "They [the leaders] just want us to be afraid all the time. And yes, there are things to be afraid of. In Israel, it's not black and white. There are some awful Arabs, just like there are some awful Israelis."

──────────── *Who Is the Warrior?* ────────────

Is it possible to resist the very human tendency to dehumanize or scapegoat whole groups of people? Listening to my interviewees and confronting the contradictions embedded in Israeli society often felt painful and confusing to me. I realized that these contradictions also lived within me: I grew up praying for the Jewish State and ardently love Israel to this day.

I looked for some answers in my ongoing conversations with Reuven, the Rumanian octogenarian who had played the harmonica during our first interview.

"You were a refugee for years, always under the heel of those who hated you, the Red Army, Antonescu's fascists, the Nazis," I noted.

"Yes, it was a difficult childhood," he agreed. "I thought that if I would write a book, my title could be: *Bilti Mitayef, the Indefatigable Refugee.* Because in my life I was expelled dozens of times."

"Yet your spirit was not vanquished. How did you come through all of those trials?

"It was a lot of trauma, but maybe by my nature, I came to different conclusions from my sufferings than others. Most draw a circle around the enemy and accuse them. But I refuse to put every person into one pool. There were a lot of good [nonJewish] people, too."

In the time of the Mishnah," Reuven continued, "it was a time of spirituality for the Jews. One of the sayings of our *Chachamim* [sages] was a question and answer. *Who is the rich person? The one who is content with what he has. Who is the wise person? One who learns from all people. Who is the warrior? The one who masters his passions.*[9]

"It is very difficult to master your passions, you know," he said with a wink. "I will give you a better answer: *Ha-hofech Oyev l'Ohev*.[10] The true warrior is the one who converts his enemy into his friend.

"Listen, if you want to understand what my life is," Reuven continued, "this is my deepest belief: To survive, we must learn to make our enemies into our friends. And you can only do this by stepping into their shoes. This is what I took out of my suffering. And I have lived like this my whole life."

"But how did you come to that conclusion?" I persisted.

"Maybe by my nature," he said again. "I came into this world not to hate but to love. Therefore, I try to bring this message everywhere possible. It is easy to hate. Much more complicated to see your enemy as your friend."

Then he added: "I was much more optimistic years ago.

"Listen, I am very sorry about the Palestinians. But they did not understand that a people like the Jewish people which went though such suffering, a people which experienced Auschwitz and Maidenik, a people that succeeded in saving itself, to say that we should throw you into the sea.[11] That was not the good strategy. This is our trauma, yes.

"Tirzah, I am sorry for this tsunami of ideas!" Reuven said with a little laugh. "One of our mistakes is that we, from the position of our own slavery, forgot. Yes, we Jews have forgotten! We who have gone through so much traumas. You know Rabbi Hillel? He was once asked, is it possible to understand the spirit of Judaism. He answered: *Don't do to the other what is hateful to you!*

"We need to resist our nature. Not to be spoiled by our victories, not to do what they did to us."

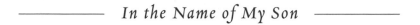

In the Name of My Son

In January 2018, I spoke with Robi Damelin, a charismatic Israeli leader whose work I had been following for years. Robi is in her seventies, a striking woman with high cheekbones and short-cropped hair. In 2002, Robi's twenty-eight-year-old son David was killed by a Palestinian sniper while serving his military reserve duty at a checkpoint. Somehow she knew instantly that David's death had presented her with a moral choice, a test of her integrity.

"When the army came to my door to tell me that David had been killed, apparently, the first thing I said was, *'You may not take revenge in the name of my son!'*" Robi said. "It was totally instinctive. I saw then that I had a choice about what to do with my pain—to invest it in revenge or try to think creatively.

"David was a student at Tel-Aviv University doing a masters in the philosophy of education. When he was called up to the reserves, he came to talk to me. 'What shall I do?' he asked, because he was in such a quandary.... But then he went, and I was filled with dread.

"He was murdered by a Palestinian sniper who, as a child, had seen his uncle killed very violently. So this man went on a path of revenge and unfortunately, David was in the way, along with nine other people.

"After [David] was killed, I was beside myself with grief. Friends from all over Israel arrived with food and drink and other little expressions of love."

Because Robi worked in Tel Aviv in public relations, word of her loss was passed on quickly, along with her declaration about revenge. Members of the Parent Circle-Families Forum (PCFF) took notice and shortly thereafter, the group's founder, Yitzhak Frankenthal, got in touch. The organization soon became her lifeline.

A few years later, Israeli army officials again knocked at Robi's door. This time they brought a message that the IDF had caught the sniper who had killed David. They asked if she wanted to attend his trial.

"I said no, because what was the point? Would it bring back David if I felt good about the fact that this man was rotting in jail and his mother is sitting alone without him? I don't believe in revenge because what revenge could I take to bring David back?

"But I am also very reluctant to use the word 'forgiving.' Does forgiving mean giving up your right to justice? Does it mean that what they did was okay, or that they can do it again? Or do you forget? I simply don't know."

Robi decided to write a letter to the family of David's killer telling them that he was a peace activist who struggled with having to serve in the occupied Palestinian territories. It was delivered to them by two Palestinian friends of hers. There was no response. And then, two and a half years later, she received a letter from David's killer himself through the Palestinian news service.

"It was not exactly a letter written by Martin Luther King," Robi said. "It was a letter filled with hate and justification for killing, telling me that my son was a murderer. The sniper said he didn't want me anywhere near his family and would not write to me directly.

"The letter upset me terribly. But I also realized through this process that I was no longer a victim, dependent upon the Palestinian sniper. The path of reconciliation brought peace to my life."

"You know, the pain doesn't go away," Robi mused. "You could take anything and everything from me, if I could only see David one more time. I think of him all the time. At the place where he is buried, the parents make beautiful gardens around the graves of their loved ones. I see it as a continuation of motherhood, the enduring need to tend to your child."

In addition to being a spokeswoman for PCFF, Robi belongs to an international organization called the Forgiveness Project.[12] And she has traveled back to her native South Africa to study the social structures that helped make reconciliation possible after fifty years of apartheid. Robi wondered if perhaps some form of that country's Truth and Reconciliation Commission could be applied to the Israeli-Palestinian conflict. While she was there, she met a woman named Ginn whose daughter had been brutally murdered twenty years earlier.

"Ginn helped me find forgiveness. She explained that forgiveness for her is 'giving up her just right for revenge.' After Ginn forgave the man responsible for killing her daughter, he told her that her forgiveness had released him from the prison of his inhumanity."

Ironically, Robi returned to Israel to learn that the Palestinian sniper who had killed David was on the list of 1,000 Palestinian prisoners "with blood on their hands" who were to be freed in exchange for the safe return of one Israeli soldier.[13]

"Once again, I was faced with a test to see if I am honest and I mean what I say," Robi said. "I sequestered myself for three days to grapple with this test. I came out knowing that David is not coming back. That no matter how many prisoners are released or kept incarcerated, David was not coming back. I know that a prisoner exchange is a part of any peace agreement. This is the way it has been the world over. This is the way for Israel, too."

PRINCIPLE FIVE

Disidentifying from Victimhood

"Don't be so stupid as to think the Goyim wouldn't slit your throat at the first opportunity. After what we went through, are you insane to defend them? Don't you understand that we are fighting for our very existence?"
—My father, Sol; taken from my high school diary

KATIA, AN ISRAELI GRADUATE STUDENT born in Russia, speaks near-perfect English with only the faintest of Israeli accents. Sitting with her in a café over steaming cups of tea, she told me the following:

"These are some of the truths I grew up with that were never questioned. *We are victims. We need to fight. They are barbaric and immoral. They have no respect for human life. You give them a finger, they will take a whole hand. We are the chosen people and the rest of the world is trying to eliminate our existence. Never forget what happened to us. If we are not actively fighting, we will be erased from the face of the earth. The worst-case scenario will happen because it already did."*

My mouth must have hung open because Katia started to laugh. She had just rattled off so many of the messages that I, an *American* Jew, had received from my own father growing up. Her list described the mindset of a people who have suffered the trauma of extreme aggression and loss, who were isolated and without resources to defend themselves, and who fear the repetition of injustice. They are the beliefs of a people who define themselves as *victims*.

And the label is justifiable. The only trouble with this self-definition and the beliefs that emerge from it is that we are left with few choices. Identifying ourselves as victims freezes our focus on the past, and therefore forecloses on our future. As victims of our history—whether of rape, persecution, or any disaster, however small or large, that leaves us helpless—even fighting back can become a fixed posture, a lifestyle. We see this in Katia's statement: *If we are not actively fighting, we will be erased from the face of the earth.*

— *The Legacy of Worldwide Anti-Semitism*[1] —

But there can be no discussion about disidentifying from Jewish victimhood without first acknowledging that Jews have, in fact, been the victims of persecution for thousands of years. Westerners might associate that victimhood with Jewish ghettos, concentration camps, and the genocide carried out by the Nazi regime. But the scourge that is commonly called anti-Semitism[2] has a much longer history and many more faces.

From the very first centuries of the last millennium, European Christendom targeted this tiny religious minority, projecting upon Jews all manner of suspicion and hatred. It is no wonder that to this day the cross is for many Jews anything but a symbol of Christian love.[3] For the hundreds of thousands of Jews along the route to Jerusalem, the Christian campaigns to the Holy Land known as the Crusades (1095-1291) were in fact, blood baths in the name of Jesus Christ. Likewise, the Spanish Inquisition, which began in the fifteenth century and was not abolished until 1834, was set up by the Catholic papacy to brutally root out, torture, expel, or kill suspected heretics.

In the sixteenth century, Martin Luther challenged Catholic dogma and changed the face of Christianity. But many Protestants are unaware that Luther was a virulent anti-Semite whose edicts caused endless torment to Jews in his century. His accusations of Jewish world rule, criminality, and plague became Adolph Hitler's playbook four centuries later.[4]

Farther East, the massacres of Jewish civilians in present-day Ukraine (1648-1657) and the relentless attacks on Jewish populations throughout the Russian Empire (from the eighteenth century through the twentieth century) became known as the pogroms. Over hundreds of years of persecution, the Jews of Europe grew to expect humiliation, forced conversions, expulsions, and annihilation for simply being themselves.

As I have discussed, anti-Jewish discrimination in Northern Africa and the Middle East was a different story, yet it was not unrelated to the European brand. Although Jews lived in relative peace under the Ottoman Empire, Arab and Jewish nationalism spurred pogroms and massacres beginning in the twentieth century.

Most of these anti-Jewish attacks were prior to the establishment of Israel in 1948, at which time massive numbers fled Arab countries. Throughout the 1930s Jews endured attacks in Algeria. In 1941, the mob violence in Bagdad was known as the Iraqi Farhud. Violent demonstrations against Jews broke out in Egypt and Libya in 1945, and in Aleppo, Syria, riots killed scores of Jews, and torched Jewish schools and synagogues in 1947.

Trying to explain Jewish scapegoating gives rise to endless theories. Most relevant to our discussion here is the reality that no matter what a Jew's ancestry or where Jews have hailed from, Jewish identity today is bound up with some facet of victimhood. Whether through family stories, media, education, or personal experience, Jewish victim identity comes to us via trauma images and sensory information deposited and carried in the bodies and minds of Jews everywhere. Without awareness, victimhood can become our central organizing principle.

So how do we honor Jewish history and the suffering that the Jewish people have endured without internalizing the harmful aspects of Jewish historical trauma and carrying them forward? Is it possible to disengage from the fear of continued persecution, helplessness, and mistrust, and claim a sense of agency? I asked several young Jews this question, and was surprised by their wisdom.

Running Out of Time

I met Sylvia at a conference where I was speaking about Jewish ancestral healing. A vivacious dark haired woman in her early thirties, Sylvia was full of stories about her family's past. I asked her to tell me about her upbringing.

"We were raised to believe that anti-Semitism is everywhere, that it's a virus in the world that never goes away," Sylvia told me. "This is how my family lived: to always be on the lookout for the hatred to resurface.

"My parents would tape newspaper clippings on our fridge so we couldn't miss the news about the latest anti-Jewish attacks around the world. It wasn't that they wanted us to feel unsafe. They just wanted us to never forget. The message was: *Don't forget that this is your lineage, this is where you come from.*"

Sylvia and her siblings were raised in a comfortable home in the Midwest. Her grandparents, Miki and Dora, were Hungarian Jews who had escaped their country in 1956, during the nationwide revolt against the Communist government and its Soviet-imposed policies. Miki and Dora and their two young sons—one of whom would become Sylvia's father—hid in the back of a fruit truck and crossed the Austrian border at night.

Fear was never far from the surface for the post-war Jewish community in Hungary. Their terror was reignited when street orators in Budapest began public rants against the Jews, and pogrom-like attacks broke out in small towns across the country. These were stark reminders of the extreme hatred that had fueled the murder and deportation of 600,000 Hungarian Jews little more than a decade earlier.

"Interestingly, it wasn't my grandparents who told us these stories, but my parents. *Don't think for a second that it couldn't happen here,* they would say. Miki and Dora, they didn't want to scare us. They were all about joy.

"But growing up, I was obsessed with the numbers on my grandmother's arm. She and her sister had been taken to Auschwitz as teenagers in 1944. Only my grandmother made it out. She was never able to resolve her guilt.

"Just before liberation, her sister got very sick in the camp. My grandmother insisted that she go get help. Her sister finally agreed to go, but she never came back. Three weeks later, Auschwitz was liberated. My poor grandmother never forgave herself for not making the right call."

"It's taken me years to work through these family legacies," Sylvia continued. "For instance, I had this deep anxiety around time. An almost visceral belief that I won't have enough time, that there's never enough time to do what I have to do. There wasn't enough time for my great aunt; I guess I internalized that. And making the wrong call—oh, there are terrible consequences to that. I had a terrible fear of ever making the wrong choice. It was paralyzing."

"My generation may be the first without any running," Sylvia added. "I mean being a refugee. After all, it's relatively safe here [in the US]. But I still feel this sense of running in my body. It's as if I've been running all my life."

Sylvia's ability to notice and track her body's messages, along with a passion for dance, took her into the field of dance therapy. She now has a thriving private practice on the West Coast helping people listen to the wisdom of their bodies and express themselves through movement. As for her family,

Sylvia knew she needed some distance before she could fully appreciate them for who they are.

"I had to move to another part of the country to see clearly. I love my family. And our history is important to me. It's who I am and I will never forget it," Sylvia told me. "But I don't want fear to control me. Even if it's true what they say, that Jews are unsafe in the world, I simply cannot live that way."

——————— *No One Is Out to Get Me* ———————

Katia, too, had found that geographical distance was a necessary ingredient in her recovery. I asked her about the journey that brought her from the Soviet Union to Sderot, Israel, and then to the United States.

"My parents' families had lived in the Soviet Union for so long, and always with heavy institutional discrimination and few opportunities. Actually, victimhood brought my family a sense of motivation," Katia said. "In that sense, it was good.

"They moved us to Israel to 'flip the script' of their victimhood. They had been so mistreated; they wanted my brother and me to have all the opportunities that they were denied.

"For example, my mother wanted very badly to study English literature in Moscow at a famous school. She passed the exam and went in for her interview. She arrived there, but once they saw her nose, they said, *Get out!*

"Her *nose?*" I asked incredulously. "Do you mean that literally?"

"Yes," Katia replied quite seriously. "My mom has a *very* Jewish nose. It gave her away. So there she was outside, walking the streets of Moscow, her beloved city, knowing that inherently, just the way she was, everything about her was in the way of receiving what she wants. Those streets she loved would never be hers. She was in a kind of jail there. When I think of that, it breaks my heart.

"The difference between us is that I see a much more beautiful world than she ever did. I'm allowed to have so much more freedom in my thoughts."

I asked Katia to tell me how she got to this freedom in her thinking.

"Well, unlike my parents, I grew up in Israel, where I was never discriminated against. Well, in the wars with the Palestinians, I guess I felt like a persecuted victim then," she added as an afterthought. "But in general, the sky was the limit there. I had so much more freedom than my mother did.

"In Israel, maybe if my skin color were different, I would be the victim of discrimination, but I 'pass,'" Katia said, drawing quote marks in the air. "I'm white. And I inherited my dad's nose!" she said with a big laugh.

"Really, two things undid the victim narrative for me," Katia went on.

"First was physical space. I knew I needed to take a break from life in Israel. But even moving to the San Francisco area didn't do it. The city was too agitated for me.

"So I took a trip to Hawaii!" she said with a grin. "There I found enough peace and tranquility [so] that I could work on myself. I would repeat: *No one is out to get me! I'm safe! I'm safe.* I had to say that again and again. Finally, it started to sink in.

"The second thing is ongoing: It's my Israeli community here in town, that I've told you about. My friends help me a lot. They call me out when I fall into my victim story. You know, that inner voice that tells me *the world is out to get me.* Or that *everything that can go wrong will go wrong.* It's an Israeli thing.

"It works because they aren't confrontational. It's an agreement we've made together. Because we all come from different parts of Israel, but we all have some version of that victim voice. We do it for each other."

Katia told me she plans to go back to Israel after she graduates. Then her thoughts took another turn. "You know, as an Israeli, I have control of my life. No one is out to arrest me and put me in jail.

"So it took me a long time to understand what life is like for a Palestinian. One day I suddenly *got* the security checkpoints, and what it means to be constantly stopped and inspected. And what it means that little kids who throw rocks on passing cars can get locked up for ten years. Israelis can lock you up and not have to answer to anyone," Katia explained.

"But in the war against victimhood, a Palestinian adult doesn't want to throw rocks anymore. They want to get control of their life. So they strap on a suicide vest. They may die, but they're no one's victim.

"You know what?" she said looking right into my eyes, "I hate this cycle! And I hate how the Palestinians celebrate their *shuhadim* [martyrs]," Katia said with a cringe. "But I understand it.

"Because a sense of victimhood justifies extreme actions. It creates a sense of righteousness.

"For example," she said after a long pause, "my parents constantly have Holocaust images in their mind. They didn't even experience the Holocaust directly, but they carry those pictures. That justifies the images they see on Israeli TV, the rough treatment of Palestinians. They say: *We Jews only want what we deserve.*"

──────── *Is It Happening Again?* ────────

In my interviews with Jews from various countries, the fear that history may be repeating itself was a recurrent theme. I understood that behind such questions as *Are Jews safe here? Could this be 1939 all over again?* lies a deep insecurity nourished by historical precedents.

In fact, recent events in Europe support such questions: The murder of a rabbi and three children in front of a Hebrew school in Toulouse, France (March 2012). A gunman shooting four people dead in front of the Jewish Museum in Brussels (May 2014). Eight months later, two days after the Charlie Hebdo murders, a gunman in Paris taking hostages in a Jewish supermarket, killing four (January 2015). In February 2015, a gunman walking into a synagogue in Copenhagen, killing one.

There is no denying or rationalizing the rise of anti-Jewish violence in Europe.[5] These events have traumatized the Jewish community on that continent and the world over.

And in the United States, the rise of anti-Jewish hate crimes[6]—the desecration of Jewish cemeteries, swastikas spray painted on public buildings, and an army of neo-Nazis carrying torches and shouting *Jews will not replace us!*—have shocked the world and retraumatized many Jews who carry within themselves images from the Jewish genocide of World War II.

In the autumn of 2018, a white supremacist from the newly empowered American radical right burst into a Pittsburgh synagogue and brutally murdered eleven congregants during Sabbath worship, seriously wounding six others, including police officers. It was the bloodiest massacre of Jews in US history, but it was by no means an isolated incident.

Organized, ideologically-driven, violent attacks against American Jews and Jewish institutions have been occurring sporadically for decades.[7] But this one, as well as the killer's hateful rants and conspiracy theories posted uncensored on social media, served to jolt the Jewish community awake. "We need to wake up to the facts," a rabbinic colleague told me the following week. "The Jewish American dream has been shattered."

Could it happen again? For Jews in the United States and in Europe, the question hangs in the air like a thought bubble. Marek, a seventy-year-old Jew from Sweden told me assuredly, "Of course it could happen. We are not safe and will never be safe as long as we are Jews." I heard this dark sentiment again and again in my interviews, both in Israel and the diaspora. As a Polish émigré to Israel put it: "We are the world's scapegoats."

Here again, we must ask: Is it possible to confront these waves of hatred, remaining aware of their magnitude, without giving oneself over to the mechanisms of retraumatization: fear, reactivity, unreason?

Even amid the voices of fatalism, the response of many American and European Jews has been instructive. "We are far more aware and powerful than in the '30s. And we have purposefully built alliances," one prominent New York City rabbi told me. "Unlike before, we stand together with our black, brown, Muslim, and Christian neighbors."

In Europe, the rise in anti-Semitic attacks on European soil might justifiably have sent Jews fleeing. Yet there has been only a partial exodus[8], less than one might imagine. Despite early reports of an uptick in Jewish immigration from Europe to Israel,[9] and despite the urgings of Israeli political officials to see these events as warnings,[10] the overwhelming majority of European Jews are choosing to remain in their home communities.

One event illustrated the situation. After the Paris kosher supermarket massacre on January 9, 2015, Israeli Prime Minister Benjamin Netanyahu visited Paris. He spoke to a packed synagogue there, urging French Jews to abandon life on the continent and "come home" to Israel.

When he finished his remarks, a remarkable thing occurred. The audience spontaneously rose to their feet and burst into "La Marseillaise," the French national anthem. Netanyahu stood by awkwardly. The audience's response was entirely unscripted.

Later, the director of the European Jewish Association commented: "The reality is that a large majority of European Jews do not plan to emigrate to Israel. The Israeli government must recognize this reality . . . and cease this Pavlovian reaction every time Jews in Europe are attacked."[11] Likewise, the Chief Rabbi of Denmark commented, "Terror is not a reason to move to Israel."[12]

For many Jews, moving to Israel, or making *aliya*, is the realization of an ultimate dream. This was the case for my own parents, who made *aliya* in 1977, fulfilling a lifelong vow to fully claim their vision of a renewed Judaism. They had planned their immigration for years before they made their way to the seaside city of Netanya, and the move was full of excitement and a profound sense of achievement for them. It is a very different thing to flee to Israel in a state of panic.

───── *Remembering Our Collective Power* ─────

Is it happening again? For those who have lived through racial violence or have inherited ancestral trauma, it is easy to fall into fear and hyperarousal at the shocking racism and violence on our streets today. For there are indeed similarities between the anti-Jewish hatred of the 1930s and '40s and more current brands of anti-Semitism.

But there are also important differences.[13] The former hatred, advanced by the Third Reich, was state-sponsored and institutionally organized at the highest levels of government, methodically carried out against Jews and other minorities.

Yes, this hatred was picked up and augmented by European gentiles—Romanians, Poles, and Austrians among them—not unlike hate-mongers in the West today who are invigorated by aggression against others, and euphoric at the possibility of easy answers. But what is occurring more recently in both Europe and the US is not promoted by one uniform movement, but is rather the projects of unassociated hate groups acting out their far-right racist ideologies in the form of independent acts of terror.

However dangerous and abhorrent these hate groups are—and their threat is not to be underestimated—it is questionable whether they pose an existential threat to Jews as did the Nazi regime. Their hate crimes are, in fact, being aimed at many minorities, refugee groups, and non-white populations, Jews being just one among them.[14]

Most important for our discussion is the shifting Jewish vantage point from helpless victimhood to public acknowledgment of the facts on the ground, coupled with a sense of collective agency. For example, studying the new reality helps us to discern that Jews are now living in an age of unprecedented freedom and agency in the West. In the United States, the American Jewish establishment represents the most powerful minority in the country's history, a political force that has the guaranteed protection of the world's mightiest army.

In Europe, the vile xenophobia that has been directed toward Jews and other minority groups arises from unstable populations that are themselves struggling for social and economic power. There is trauma on every side of racial and social lines, and in the violence that results, we all lose a piece of our humanity. Jews are not the only ones asking: *Why should I be hated for something I cannot help but be?* But Jews, because of their long history of persecution, can call on that history to see, understand, and act.

———— *Agency and the Search for Meaning* ————

Another key to trauma recovery is *agency,* the inner sense that we are in charge of our lives and can shape its outcome. Quite the opposite are the feelings of helpless victimization that continuous oppression imprints upon bodies and minds. For much of Jewish history, Jews had no agency in the larger world, no possibility for shaping their outward circumstances, and no reprieve from the continuous victimization that was the Jew's lot.

Seeking power after victimization might naturally lead to taking action to defend ourselves and our communities from further harm. This power may at times become forceful, even violent, in the quest for justice. But an important distinction is that while agency is always powerful, not all forms of power are synonymous with agency.

Simply put, agency is not reactive. As Viktor Frankl taught, it comes from self-awareness. Because even when overt action is impossible or unwise, we can still have agency; we can still own our sense of self, and the meaning that we alone assign to our lives.

Agency always awaits our finding. In Frankl's terms, our ability to find meaning cannot be taken away from us. It is "the last of human freedoms—to choose one's attitude in any given set of circumstances, to choose one's own way."[15]

In so many of my interviews—with young and old, first-, second-, and third-generation Jewish survivors of trauma—the sense of agency was intertwined with the search for a larger meaning. Rather than identify with the trauma legacy that their tragedy had left them—feelings of fatalism, fear, and victimization—their focus turned to the struggle to "make sense out of a senseless thing," as Rami put it after losing his fourteen-year-old daughter in a terrorist attack. For him and many others, meaning was found in reaching beyond their singular suffering to the suffering of others, to prevent others, however possible, from enduring the traumas that they themselves had endured. In this reach lay their agency.

——————— *Two Kinds of Jews* ———————

I invited Avner over one morning to discuss what was most meaningful to him. On an earlier occasion, this strapping twenty-nine-year-old Israeli army reservist had told me about the impact of his experiences as an IDF officer serving in the occupied Palestinian territories. On this particular day, Avner wanted to tell me about the legacy his grandfather had given him.

"My grandfather is a very smart man," Avner told me over tea in my rented apartment in Jerusalem. "Apart from other things, he is also a history professor and taught for years at Cornell. One of the things he taught me is the idea that out of the ashes of the Holocaust arose two kinds of Jews with two different perspectives.

"One kind of Jew says: *The Holocaust happened to us as Jews and we have to do whatever we can, with whatever means, to make sure it does not happen to us as Jews ever again.*

"If you listen to the rhetoric of certain people here [in Israel], you will hear this view a lot. It's always about the Holocaust. For them, disaster is once again just around the corner. For them, Jews are all alone. We can't trust the Europeans. Look what they did to us! And how can the Germans criticize us? Look what *they* did to us!

"The second kind of Jew—and this is the kind of Jew that I want to be—is the Jew that says: *We were part of one of the biggest catastrophes that happened in humanity. We were one of the groups that were harmed from this, but not the only group, and we now have the responsibility that this will never happen to anyone again.*

"These are the two, and that's the big difference, I would say. You see it clearly in the back-and-forths on Facebook. And you see it underlying all the political discussions in this country. Now, with African refugees and asylum seekers [entering Israel], it's coming up again. People say: *They are taking our jobs. Taking our places.*

"Now, that's textbook World War II anti-Semitism. But then you have the people who say: *We have a responsibility, we who were refugees.* Now, that is the kind of Jew I want to be," Avner declared.

PRINCIPLE SIX

Redefining Jewish Chosenness

"If we are chosen, then chosen for what?"
—Reuven, Holocaust Survivor

ONE OF THE TROUBLESOME RESIDUES of the anti-Semitic trauma legacy is the identity of *otherness* that it has generated in many Jews, the subtle yet pervasive sense that Jews are somehow different, alien, and unwelcome in this world. But complicating the identity of *otherness* is a second core message, one that is intrinsic to the very foundations of Judaism: the belief that Jews are the chosen people.

The idea that Jews are special, unique, and set apart by God for an uncommon destiny stems from the Hebrew Bible, or Torah, which was compiled around the sixth century BCE, based upon oral teachings many hundreds of years older. At the very inception of Jewish nationhood, just after the

Hebrew tribes were liberated from Egyptian bondage, God declares that they shall be *"My own treasure from among all peoples...a kingdom of priests and a holy nation"* (Exod. 19:5-6). Soon afterwards, Moses declares, *"You are a nation set apart for God your God who chose you to be His special people from all the nations on the face of the earth"* (Deut. 7:6).

Centuries later, the prophet Isaiah would designate the Israelites as *"a light unto the nations"* (Is. 49:6, 42:6, 60:3). And Isaiah's contemporary, the prophet Amos, would declare: *"You alone have I singled out from all the families of the earth"* (Am. 3:2).

———— *Please Choose Somebody Else* ————

A dubious gift, indeed! Jewish chosenness may sound like a privilege on parchment, but it has elicited anything but reverence and goodwill from the many "unchosen" on the face of the earth. As the Yiddish writer Shalom Aleichem said, in the voice of the character Tevye in *Fiddler on the Roof*: *"God, I know we are your chosen people, but couldn't you choose somebody else for a change?"*

Humor helps when dealing with a legacy of tragedy and persecution. "Just look at Jewish history," said comedian Mel Brooks. "Unrelieved lamenting would be intolerable. So, for every ten Jews beating their breasts, God designated one of us to be crazy, so we can amuse the breast-beaters. By the time I was five, I knew I was that one."

As I learned in my work with both religious and secular Jews, chosenness means radically different things to different people. Jews feel a subtle or not so subtle sense of entitlement as one of "God's chosen people." As one client confessed to me: "I was raised to think that Jews are different and special. I'm embarrassed by that now, but I still carry a secret sense of hubris. Or maybe I should call it, *Hebris*."

Jews have much to be proud of: their people's standards of educational excellence, their business and musical acumen, their tradition of philanthropy, and a disproportionate number of Nobel Prize laureates. And often transcending all others is pride in the fact that Jews have survived every attempt to wipe them out, and are still thriving today as one of the oldest civilizations on the face of the earth.

Yet deeply interwoven with this sense of self-esteem, many Jews also carry a persistent sense of being predestined for trouble. We might understand this unease as the post-traumatic residue of centuries of life under pernicious ruling dynasties and governments. Jews have had a proverbial bag packed for hundreds of years, ready for the next expulsion, anticipating the next crisis.

Hyperarousal has indeed been warranted. But chronic vigilance, born of Jewish history and integral to Jewish identity, keeps people from seeing themselves or raising their children as truly safe members on this earth. Hyperarousal means being always on edge, on the periphery, vigilant for trouble, and reading signs of disaster on the horizon and in the tea leaves. Knowledge of history and the desire to survive demand this. The dual identity of *other* and chosen keeps the trauma narrative alive and active.

─────────── *An Unbearable Burden* ───────────

Is chosenness exclusively Jewish? Of course not. Each of the three monotheistic religions make a unique claim to divine election.[1] Erik Erikson, one of the twentieth century's most influential developmental psychologists, noted that many of the world's castes, tribes, nations, and religions "provide their members with a sense of God-given identity," causing them to "behave as if they were a separate species created at the beginning of time by supernatural intent."[2]

Still, Judaism has specialized in specialness. The very idea was intrinsic to the mythic structure of this ancient tradition, both in relationship with the non-Jewish world, as well as within its own social order. In the earliest records of ancient Judaism (for example, as spelled out in the Book of Leviticus), we find that hierarchy was built into the legal, religious, and social orders, granting priority of males over females, priests over Levites, and Levites over other Israelites. And at the level of family, the primogeniture or firstborn son had special status over the other children, being honored with special blessings and a double inheritance from his father's estate.[3]

In a postmodern world, these ancient hierarchies have all but been dissolved, at least in non-Orthodox circles. Today the priestly castes are symbolically honored, but in the absence of the Temple in Jerusalem, have no substantive function. And in many Jewish communities around the world, the implicit biblical value that men are the normative Jew has given way to a more egalitarian worldview. Women are now scholars, rabbis, cantors, and leaders of equal (or near-equal) voice, and are changing the landscape of Jewish communal practice. Likewise, daughters—firstborn and otherwise—are finding their own place of honor and value, and are welcomed into the community with rituals that parallel those of baby boys and young men.

Nevertheless, the status of males, and in particular, the veneration of the firstborn male, *bachor* in Hebrew, still lingers, embedded in the mythic origins of the Jewish people and recalled at every Passover table around the world.

In the Passover narrative of the ten plagues (Exod. 11:5, 12:12), God's dark angel struck down every firstborn human and animal male in Egypt in order to weaken the Pharaoh's grip on the Israelite slaves. The angel however "passed over" the doorways of all Jewish firstborn males on that fateful night, sparing them. From that day forward, all Israelite firstborn males were dedicated to God "*because all firstborn males are Mine,*" God declared (Num. 3:13).

This means that the God of the Israelites (whose masculinity was presumed) acquired a kind of "title" to firstborn males by virtue of having spared them. To this day, religious Jews engage in a ritual enactment known as *Pidyon HaBen*, in which a father buys back his *bachor* from God—via a priest—shortly after birth. Additionally, on the day before Passover, firstborn sons traditionally fast or study all day in commemoration of the night of the Exodus when they were spared by the Angel of Death.[4] In these ways, firstborn Jewish sons pay their dues to the God who saved them, and by so doing, owns them.[5]

Most secular Jews know little of the Jewish "cult of the firstborn." Nevertheless, the fact that certain members of a family carry an innate specialness—that they *belong to God*—creates a pressure that is subtle yet profound.

Most pointedly, in regard to Jewish historical trauma, specialness accorded even at the smallest social stratum, within the circle of the family, reinforces the larger theme of hierarchy and chosenness as a people. At all levels, the notion of divine election creates an unbearable burden: to fulfill a destiny that demands obedience and superhuman excellence.

———————— *Ancestral Pressure* ————————

This was the case in my own family. At the end of the nineteenth century, my mother's two grandfathers each left their homes to travel across Hungary to attend the most influential yeshiva of prewar Europe. There they studied together under the *helige Chasam Sofer*,[6] the greatest legal authority of the day, known for his impeccable orthodoxy.

The two became best friends, and betrothed their children—my mother's parents—to be married. My great-grandparents spent their lives advancing Judaism and creating Jewish educational institutions in what is now the Czech Republic and Slovakia. They died in the late 1920s, just before the Third Reich rose to power.

In June 2016, my sister Laya and I visited their graves in the tiny towns of Uhersky Brod and Topolcany, whose Jewish denizens were all deported to Theresienstadt and Auschwitz by the Nazis. We were overwhelmed with joy to find that our great-grandparents' headstones were still standing. We never expected to find them resting in shady, well-kept Jewish cemeteries, tended by local gentiles who keep them safe under lock and key.

These Christian guardians know well what happened to their Jewish neighbors. In both towns, the synagogues have been turned into museums that show the history of the Jewish communities there.

As my sister and I walked in the towns where our ancestors are buried, looked at photographs, and listened to the stories of today's inhabitants, I imagined these places as they once were, teeming with Jewish life. Kneeling by our great-grandparents' graves, I sensed the absence of all those who never had the privilege of burial. And I understood all the more the ancestral pressure—and my own parents' dogged will—to recreate a way of life that had been crushed by the Nazis.

Danny

My eldest brother Danny was born in the first days of 1944 while the war still blazed in Europe and my father, then stationed with his new bride in Salt Lake City, waited on standby for deployment. As the *bachor,* Danny inherited the duty to repair and continue the chain of European Torah scholarship that had been all but broken. In our family, we were all charged with the work of bringing Judaism back to life again. But our eldest brother, more than any of us, bore the weight of this responsibility.

Danny showed signs of intellectual brilliance from his earliest years. At the Telshe Yeshiva, where rigorous Talmud study was the gold standard, he stood out. The rabbis' eyes were upon him as a future rabbi, perhaps an heir apparent.

In those days, Danny, who was more than ten years my senior, was a god to me. I was euphoric when he arrived home for visits from his yeshiva boarding school, and I would follow him around the house. He didn't seem to mind.

Danny confided to me that he saw otherworldly lights dancing over the Hebrew letters of his Talmud as he studied late into the night. He also shared his quandary over girls. Surrounded by males day and night in the yeshiva, and prohibited from any contact with females his age, how would he ever get to know them? I listened avidly to every word. But even as a little girl, I sensed a crash was coming.

When Danny was eighteen, something snapped. He began to question the Orthodox system, then to doubt. He knew instinctively that to have a shot at living his own life, he needed to get outside the walls of the parochial yeshiva setting. Most of all, he knew he needed out from the overpowering onus of his role as the "golden boy," the firstborn son who would redeem his Jewish ancestors.

Danny made an appointment with his headmaster and told him that he wanted to leave the yeshiva to study philosophy at the university. Several years later, Danny told me what his rabbi had said.

"Daniel, a boy like you? You were meant to be an important scholar! That is the greatest thing a Jew can do with his life. After so many were lost, *gevalt!* We must build back what has been destroyed, not betray it!"

After arguing for some time and seeing that he was getting nowhere, the rabbi finally said: "Listen to me, Daniel. If you follow this path, there will be trouble. You won't live past thirty. *I'm telling you now. You won't live past thirty!*"

Danny took the dare. He put himself through college and graduate school and became an untenured professor in classics and biblical criticism at the state university. But as if living out the rabbi's words, Danny never flourished. He lived an isolated life; his face wore the cynicism of a man twice his age.

At age twenty-seven, my brother came across *Three Pillars of Zen* by Philip Kapleau. The book gripped him, stumping his quick mind and inviting him into a transcendent vista that he longed for. For the first time since leaving yeshiva, Danny's parched soul seemed to have found living water.

Danny quit his teaching job and moved to Kapleau's monastery in Rochester, New York, living off savings and diving full-bore into Zen life. This meant many hours of sitting meditation a day, and austerities that even his yeshiva life had not prepared him for. He and I exchanged occasional letters. I could tell he was lonely, though completely dedicated.

Our parents were aghast. After several initial efforts to get Danny out of this place they deemed a temple of *avoda zara*, idol worship, our parents cut him off. They could not cope with their disappointment and disgrace, and they lacked either the psychological tools or the desire to understand their eldest son's choices.

As it was with Shulamith, Sol and Kate's parental love was bound up in their expectations. The only child they could accept was an Orthodox Jew, they would say, and especially their *bachor*, who had such special promise.

Two-and-a-half years later, a few months after his thirtieth birthday, our parents received a call from the sheriff in Grants County, New Mexico. A body had been found on the Native American reservation with the presumed identity of Daniel Firestone. The death was recorded as a suicide.

—————— *The Curse of the Chosen* ——————

I was twenty when Danny died, and I was overcome with grief. For many months I railed against my family and the insanely high bar that had toppled him. It took me much longer to understand that Danny had fallen under a kind of curse, *the curse of the chosen*: the impossibility of leaving the tribe and the unbearable burden of staying.

The heartless absurdity of it repelled me; I fled from Judaism and stayed away for a full decade. But Danny's curse was also the reason I eventually felt compelled to return to the tribe, to work to transform it.

My family had thrown down the gauntlet. It was mine to pick up. I felt obliged to confront a tradition that felt like a crushing, ancient monolith, to search for the truth within it, and most of all, to recover the human dimension that lay flattened and voiceless beneath the weight of our outsized traumatic history.

Upon my return, I discovered that the Jewish path contains much life-giving medicine. Nor is it monolithic, but full of divergent voices, interpretations, and room for innovation. I understood that Judaism had survived not only by dint of its adherence to law and custom, but because of its ability to evolve and adapt to whatever conditions Jews were subjected, however challenging.

—————— *The Fine Line* ——————

Over a decade of traveling to and from Israel, interviewing scores of people, and immersing myself in Israeli culture, I discovered that a literal interpretation of chosenness is still alive and quietly ubiquitous among Jews there. To my great surprise, the biblical term, *am nivchar*, chosen people, came up again and again in my everyday encounters.

In 2013 I was invited to take part in a seminar on the early socialist years of Israel. It was an excellent daylong course taught in Hebrew. As I was the only non-Israeli in the room and I am less than fluent in conversational Hebrew, I struggled to keep up.

About halfway through the seminar, the instructor asked participants to share their views with a partner. I turned to face a retired university professor in her mid-seventies. She spoke Hebrew slowly for my sake.

"We are, after all, *am ha-nivchar* [the chosen people], and ultimately that will be the prevailing truth here in Israel," she said.

"*Slichah?* Pardon me?" I stammered. "My Hebrew is weak. Perhaps I didn't understand correctly. Did you say...?"

"You heard me the first time," the woman said bluntly, switching to heavily accented English. "We are *am ha-nivchar.* The chosen people of God."

I nodded politely and made a note of it.

On another occasion, en route to Ben Gurion Airport, I conversed in English with my thirty-something-year-old taxi driver who wore a *kippah* and jeans. We chatted away about life in Jerusalem, his wife's American relatives, and their new baby. As we neared the airport, I asked him if he could explain the walls that I was seeing on either side of the highway.

"You don't want to know who lives behind those walls," he answered. "Here live all Arabs. We don't dare go in there. It's very dangerous. That's why the walls."

"When will it ever end?" I asked with a sigh.

"It won't end," he answered sharply, looking back at me through his rearview mirror, "not until the Messiah comes. That will be the end of them."

"What?" I was astonished by what this young man was saying. "Don't you think the Messiah will care about those people too?" I managed. "Surely the Messiah will bring peace to all the people of the world, not just the Jews."

"No, the Messiah is coming just for us, *am hanivchar*. No one else."

The conversation ended there. But that night, peering down on the lights of Tel Aviv from my airplane window, I understood how the idea of Jewish chosenness could fuel a social attitude that was antithetical to the humane Judaism that I had grown to love. A Judaism that instructed its people time and again to care for the stranger in its midst.

And, yes, as Tamara had told me, *there are things to be afraid of. In Israel, it's not black and white.* After decades of war and bloodshed, peace talks and shattered dreams, the chaos of terrorism, and the complexity of multi-national intervention, I understood that today Jewish trauma is finely interwoven with Palestinian trauma; and the overlapping fields of cultural injury are doubly charged with residue and reactivity.

That night I heard myself saying: *Human dignity is the most precious value, and it has been compromised. But that fact does not cancel out our responsibility and the prophetic mandate for justice.*

It occurred to me how dangerously fine the line was between chosenness and racial supremacy. Taken as religious mandate, an identity of chosenness implies a racial bias. It sanctions seeing oneself as superior; it denies the equality and dignity of other peoples, races, and voices. The self-definition of chosenness—by Jews or any other people—then becomes lethal. Under its edict, anything may be allowed.

────────── *A Single Hair* ──────────

On the last day of July in 2015, a band of Jewish extremists entered the Palestinian village of Douma before dawn. They broke a window in a home and threw in Molotov cocktails. An eighteen-month-old infant burned to death that morning and both parents later died. Before they fled, the invaders spray-painted graffiti reading "revenge" and "long live the Messiah" in Hebrew.[7]

The incident was not an isolated one. It followed a series of so-called "Price Tag" crimes carried out by a gang of religious zealots[8]— beatings and killings of unarmed Palestinian civilians, destruction of Palestinian property, and arson attacks on mosques, churches, and Arab homes.

In an article in *Haaretz*, Israeli journalist and analyst Gideon Levy tied the crimes to the doctrine of Jewish chosenness that he believes underlies Israeli Jewish society. "No principle in Israel society is more destructive, or more dangerous than this principle," Levy wrote. "Nor, unfortunately, more common."

He quoted Jewish right-wing activist Baruch Marzel, who had proclaimed that it was permissible to kill thousands of Palestinians in order to protect a single hair from the head of a Jew. "At the end of a terrible day," Levy wrote in the days after the death of the baby, "it is this [principle] that leads to the burning of families whom God did not choose.... When [chosenness] is a fundamental principle, the next torching is only a matter of time."[9]

────── *Our Myths Define Our Values* ──────

Hearing these stories, I mused to myself that perhaps in the mythic structure of the Jewish covenantal relationship with the Divine, there grew up a misunderstanding. A subtle and now not so subtle superiority had crept in, in reciprocal relationship to the relentless scapegoating that Jews had experienced.

A justifiable mistake! What were Jews chosen for, after all? Some would find it difficult to accept a Jewish mandate to care for and illuminate a world that had so mistreated them. "Was there a positive side of the *treasured nation* identity?" I asked this question of some of the interviewees who had raised the topic.

Reuven, the octogenarian survivor from Rumania, had also spent time thinking about Jewish chosenness. He told me: "The idea that Judaism was and has to be a pure lineage is a very, very dangerous idea. God never meant that we are the only one who is special, but [to live] as a model, as an *ohr lagoyim* [a light to the nations]."

Daniela, who had lost her son Tom in an Israeli military accident, commented: "Most people here [in Israel] say we are just fine! We are the best! We are *am segulah, am nivchar* [a treasured nation, a chosen people.] The Jewish soul is more important than the soul of a *Goy* [non-Jew]. All kinds of crazy things."

Daniela continued: "I told my daughter just last night as we were watching the news, maybe things [will] go into very difficult places, even fascism together with religion." She closed her eyes and shook her head for a moment. Then she looked into my eyes and exclaimed, "Wow, this is difficult stuff! But I believe the human spirit will win in the end. In the end, the human spirit wants freedom."

In the spring of 2013, in a garden overlooking Jerusalem, I spoke with a rabbinic student named Amichai about the deeply interiorized myths that keep the Jewish people bound up in suffering. He is another son who carries the heavy mantle of his lineage.

Amichai hails from a long line of rabbis. His grandfather was fifty years old when he led his congregation to the gas chambers of Treblinka with a Torah scroll in his arms. Amichai's father and uncle made a miraculous escape. Today his proud Jerusalem family is famed for its survival of the Nazi regime, and celebrated for its spiritual leadership in Israeli society.[10]

Finding himself undeniably gay in the orthodox world in Jerusalem opened for Amichai the reality of the *other*. His break from his family's religious community was enormously painful, he told me, but it freed him to think differently about many things.

After kibitzing for a few minutes and sharing second-generation survivor quirkiness, Amichai took a big breath and grew serious. He told me that he began to question collective Jewish beliefs at an early age.

"The myths we tell and how we tell them define our values," Amichai explained. "We [Jews] are recycling the story of the firstborn, and we are recycling our traumatic reactions, and we are forever Isaac on that mountain with the patriarchy at our throat with a knife!"

"You know the night I really got it?" he asked me with wide-eyed intensity. "The night Yitzchak Rabin died. I was sitting on my roof in Jerusalem looking down. That year I was studying the sacrifice of Yitzchak,[11] and I was obsessed with rewriting the text of Abraham going up to the mountain to worship."

"Right," I filled in. "Abraham is taking his beloved son Isaac [Yitzchok] to sacrifice him on the mountain. He believes he has heard God ordering him to do it."

"Yes, and I asked myself," Amichai continued. "*What if Yitzchak says no? And what if Abraham changes his mind? And what if Sarah steps in? And what if Ishmael shows up...* a lot of midrashim [new legends] were coming to me.

"That night [after hearing of Yitzchok Rabin's assassination] I thought: *Akedat Yitzchak just happened again! The sacrifice of the son just happened all over again! And this is the sequel!* Yigal Amir [the assassin] said: *God spoke to me!* And he killed Yitzchok [Rabin]! Only this time, no angel intervened!

"Our stories are wide awake and alive!" Amichai cried. "And we are perpetuating them, unless we pause and get into the stories and start futzing with them so they can go elsewhere."

Chosen for What?

Ironically, carrying the designation of "chosen people" requires a choice. What will Jews do with their mythical identity, born of prophetic proclamation and a lifetime of wandering? How will Jews' long and complex history of ethnic persecution and astonishing accomplishments create a living narrative for future generations to live by?

In my interviews with scores of Jews from around the world, I heard that the two self-definitions that Jews carry—*otherness* and chosenness—present a spiritual double bind. Used together, the two can become a wall that limits, separates, and isolates. Alternatively, the two can be woven into a narrative that gives purpose and serves as a bridge to the world, to reach those in need of compassion from a place of firsthand knowing.

We have seen how an individual or group that remains unwitting to the natural results of their trauma can unconsciously recreate the mirror image of their own suffering elsewhere. Dangers lie ahead for those who live with numbed feelings, hypervigilant reactivity, and the tendency to isolate from the world in shame or in pride.

But the work of trauma recovery can also lead to a new self-awareness. Compassion can be awakened, first for oneself and then for others.[12] Then the legacy of chosenness becomes not exclusionary, but a point of connection to a world that is suffering, and to the deepest strata of human understanding and empathy. Then one can approach the world—even one's stated enemies—with the wise voice that reminded the Jewish tribes again and again in the aftermath of oppression: *Do not oppress a stranger, for you know the heart of a stranger, for you yourselves were strangers in a harsh land.*

Ever philosophical, Reuven waxed prophetic: "Not everyone understands the spirituality of Judaism. That to be chosen is not to be superior. Not to be arrogant. On the contrary, it is to be humble, and responsible for others. I say [it means] to take our own history and convert it into kindness. Now that would make Isaiah's eyes light up!" he said with a grin.

PRINCIPLE SEVEN

Taking Action

Had I not fallen, I could not have arisen.
Had I not sat in the darkness, I could not have beheld the light.
—Midrash[1]

WHAT WILL WE DO WITH our legacies? Whether we are Jews or members of any other tribe that has suffered the trauma of genocide or persecution simply for being who we are, we must ask this question. Will we "sink into the inevitability of our inherited nightmares," as Israeli researcher Natan Kellermann warns?[2] Or will we choose to find our own unique path to transform our inheritance and give new meaning to our peoples' tragedies?

The science of epigenetics now demonstrates what many of us have suspected: that we carry a kind of "biological memory" of historical events that precede us. But we receive more than our forebears' painful legacies. We also receive the capacity to reshape the trajectory of our own lives. We can choose to work with our "givens," to override the negative effects of our painful legacies and maximize our strengths. We can transform the imprint of our ancestors' trauma.

This is the paradox: Trauma changes us in permanent and enduring ways. But we have a choice about the outcome of our story. We can bemoan our fate as victims of history. Or we can recognize our pain and follow the circumstances of our lives into unforeseen directions and new meanings. We can ask: What does this terrible wound inspire me to do that I would never have thought to do otherwise?

For Tamara, an Israeli mother who lost her son Idor in a military accident, it happened in this way. After she quit her job to give herself the energy to mourn fully, her life went into uncharted territory.

"I did therapy for two years after Idor was killed," Tamara told me. "I wasn't depressed, but just on a lower key of life. Then something unexpected happened. I had an idea, an absolute *eureka!* I said to my husband: 'I'm going to London for three months. I just need a change, and I don't want anybody else around.'"

Tamara found a tiny flat on the Internet, packed two thick volumes of *The History of Israel* and left her family behind. Once in London, she walked for miles every day, went to markets, plays, the library. In the evenings she would sit and read.

"But there happened to be an Oxfam store next door to my flat," Tamara continued. "And I am mad about secondhand stores and charities. So I volunteered there. The people who ran it became my people, my new family.

"At the end of the three months, I came back to Israel and opened a charity shop. I called it *From Door to Door—Mi Dor l'Dor* in Hebrew, which means *from generation to generation.* This was so meaningful to me because my son's name was *Idor!* My husband and I made it into a nonprofit that served the community, an *amuta,* as we call it in Hebrew.

"It became one of the most significant things of my life. And I think it changed me. I was doing something meaningful for me, for the family, for Idor. He lived on through my work."

—————— *The Prelude to Action* ——————

For every person I interviewed, finding purpose and taking action after tragedy was central to recovery. It did not seem to matter how small or large the act. For Timna, the Israeli student whose family came from Egypt, the simple act of inviting other Mizrahi students to a support group galvanized her healing process. For Sheldon, born in a displaced persons (DP) camp in Germany, it was learning about his lost family and making a film about their war experiences. And for Robi, it meant returning to her native South Africa to study the possibility of forgiveness.

But for each of them, tending the inner self was the foundation for these outward steps. Without this inner work, we may be giving our trauma new clothes, while continuing to suffer within. This was the case for Avi, the Israeli war hero who had lived on the streets of Krakow as a child.

As we saw in Chapter Three, Avi found purpose in making *aliya* and dedicating his life to the survival of his new country.

He became celebrated for his bravery and his fearless efforts, which saved many of his comrades' lives. Nonetheless, his extreme feelings of helplessness and anxiety continued for over three decades. He was tormented by a recurring dream of being ground up at the end of a conveyer belt that he could not escape. Despite his outward heroism, some part of Avi still felt like a helpless victim, a sign that his childhood trauma was still unprocessed.

When we overlook our suffering, our actions will likely bear the hallmarks of the trauma we are fleeing. In Avi's case, this meant a life of fight or flight on the battlefield, and extreme isolation and inner torment at home. By choosing to confront his pain and tell his story, Avi finally stepped off the conveyer belt. His anxiety then turned into what he calls "a wonderful sense of fulfillment and satisfaction." For Avi, the most heroic step was to allow his vulnerability to be witnessed by others.

Again, for almost every person I studied, going through some form of "dark night of the soul" preceded finding meaningful work in the world. Facing what happened, deeply mourning their losses, and following the circuitous river of emotions came first.

This very personal work cannot be bypassed or rushed. It is a necessary prelude to outward action. Without it, we will be hard-pressed to summon the energy to move forward into the world.

But in the ripeness of time—and for each person the timing is different—there is an internal readiness. Then, organically growing out of the circumstances of our lives—like Tamara, who suddenly noticed the thrift store next door—we start to *see things* in the world around us. Our environment and the events of our lives begin to speak to us, to unfold spontaneously in ways that we could not have predicted. And we find that we have a personal affinity for certain things, sometimes even a passion.

This was true in my own life. After my brother Danny committed suicide, I nursed my wounds for several years. I began Jungian analysis and journaling and practiced Tai Chi and massage therapy. Then, still in my twenties, I began to notice that the issue of suicide was arriving unbidden at my doorstep. First an acquaintance whose father had killed himself, then a co-worker's partner—it began like that.

I found myself caring for others who had lost loved ones to suicide, counseling friends who were having suicidal fantasies, writing letters to bereaved family members who were suffering this unique grief that I knew so well. My own tragedy had given me special entry into places where others could not go. I knew this territory firsthand, and therefore I could be trusted to help others through it. It was as if the world had recruited me for this special purpose.

―――――― *Just a Human in the Street* ――――――

In the spring of 2013, I met Rami in an empty restaurant in Beit Jala, not far from Bethlehem. Rami had lost his fourteen-year-old daughter, Smadar, in 1997. She and several of her friends had been out shopping when a suicide bomber detonated himself on Ben Yehuda Street in Jerusalem.

After we had talked over tea, Rami invited me to come listen to a presentation he was giving with his Palestinian counterpart, Mazen Faraj. They were in Beit Jala that evening, representing the Parents Circle-Families Forum (PC-FF), the nongovernmental organization composed of Israeli and Palestinian families who share the common bond of lost family members in the ongoing regional conflict.

I will never forget that evening and how it shook me. Rami and Mazen stood together at the head of a crowded hall. First Mazen spoke. He told of being born in the Dheisheh Refugee Camp in the West Bank, one of five brothers.

"One day in 1979, I was just four or five years old, I saw Israeli soldiers in my house. I remember it to this day. They came and took my big brother to jail.... Then another one, the second one, he went to jail the next year; and then the third one, the fourth, and the fifth. All my brothers."

In 1990, during the First Intifada, Mazen went to jail for the first time at the age of fifteen. "That first day, they just put me in a small place: less than one meter. They called it something like a temporary investigation. They shouted at me and beat me. They sometimes let me stand for five or six days without eating or drinking, without a bathroom. Just standing in the sun." Typical of young Palestinian men, Mazen was in and out of Israeli jail for several years. Prison became his university training.

"I read many, many books while I was there: history, religion, about Christians, Jews, Muslims, Qur'an, Torah, about philosophy, about Marx, about Lenin, about Descartes. Because we had a lot of time, we dealt with jail as a big university. I used the time. I did not waste it."

In April 2002, during the Second Intifada, Mazen's sixty-two-year-old father, Ali Faraj, was shot by Israeli soldiers as he walked back into the West Bank from work in Jerusalem, carrying groceries for the family. That evening his family received a call from the hospital. His father was dead. He had more than sixty bullet holes in his body.

"He did not have any gun. He did not have any stone. He did not have any fault," Mazen said, peering into our eyes. "Just a human in the street.

"I had to think about the Israelis. They killed my father. I have to, maybe to [take] revenge. Maybe I have to kill the Israelis. But also I [thought] about how that soldier killed my father not because he was my father. It was just because he was a Palestinian."

In 2005, after three years of wrestling with the immensity of his pain, Mazen joined the Parent Circle-Families Forum (PCFF).

"So I have to fight with the Palestinians against the Israelis. I chose to fight the nonviolent way. To tell them how much the occupation is bad, how much living in a camp is bad. How bad it is to live in these two worlds: allowed, and not allowed. So all my work since that time until now is to tell the Israelis the facts on the ground and to choose."

We Are Not Doomed

When it was Rami's turn to speak, he stood before us, first in silent recognition of his friend's words. Then he went on to recount how the death of his beloved daughter had led him to see in completely new ways.

It was 1998, and Rami had agreed to come to a gathering of bereaved parents that called itself the Parent Circle-Families

Forum. He had stood watching, first with skepticism, then in awe, as a busload of Israelis and Palestinians descended from the vehicle together.

"From that moment, I devoted my life in every way possible to anyone who wants to listen, and to people who do not want to listen, to convey this very basic, very simple message which says: *We are not doomed!*" Rami cried with a voice full of anguish and ardor. "This is *not our destiny* to keep on killing people in this Holy Land of ours forever! It's not written anywhere, and we can change it! We can break once and for all the endless cycle of violence and revenge and retaliation.

"And there is only one way to do it," he continued gently. "This is simply by talking to each other. Because it will not stop unless we talk."

I learned from Rami that our personal suffering can become our training ground. Where our heart is broken, we can feel the suffering of others. Reaching out from the place of our greatest vulnerability can become our greatest strength, our gift to the world.

Rami had followed his heartbreak to his new purpose; the PCFF became his life passion. In 2016, Rami became the Israeli coexecutive director with Mazen by his side as Palestinian coexecutive director. Like brothers, the two men have made their friendship and their work the cornerstones of their lives.

"So we go around the country and around the world, from people to people, from heart to heart," Rami continued. "And we tell them that our blood is exactly the same color, our pain is exactly the same pain, and our tears are just as bitter. And if we who paid the highest price can talk to one another, then anyone can, and anyone should."

——————— *Beyond Tragedy* ———————

I learned from Rami, Mazen, and scores of others, that some people who survive extreme trauma and undergo enormous psychological struggles, are ultimately changed in radically positive ways. Researchers have named this Post-Traumatic Growth (PTG).[3] As they are quick to point out, it is not the traumatic events themselves that create the growth, but how we struggle with those events and make meaning of them.

Researchers have identified several factors that are associated with PTG, including having a spiritual belief system, social support, and finding acceptance for what has occurred. And some researchers identify compassion and altruism as facets of PTG. As one study remarked: "When people recognize their own vulnerability, they may be better able to feel compassion and that some trauma may be a kind of empathy training. Out of this...may come a need to help."[4]

Rachel Yehuda agrees. "Not all effects of trauma are negative," she reminds us. Yehuda is professor of psychiatry and neuroscience and director of the Traumatic Stress Studies Division at the Icahn School of Medicine at Mount Sinai Hospital in New York. Born in Israel and educated in the United States, her groundbreaking research has focused upon children of Holocaust survivors and the epigenetic effects of mass trauma.

"The Jewish culture and religion has understood that children bear the burden of their parents' legacy. Fair or unfair, it's a fact. It's a cultural fact. It's a biological fact. Everyone is born with a unique set of genes. The task is to refine from these traits the best self that we can have and not get distracted by the traits that are weaker. Build up the traits that are stronger. We all have the same job to do."

"What you have represented among children of Holocaust survivors," Yehuda continued, "is a preponderance of people that are in therapeutic professions—doctors, nurses, social workers, psychologists. You have an extraordinarily large number of people that go into *tikkun olam,* fixing what's broken. I think that that's also a response to a cultural trauma. You can get stuck in the legacy of victimization, or you can say, 'No, no, no, no, no. I'm going to be part of the solution.'"[5]

Nevertheless, even within post-traumatic growth (PTG), complexities may be found. In a study done after the Second Intifada, reports of both Jewish and Arab reactions to violence and terrorism showed that PTG was associated with heightened PTSD.[6] It was also associated with greater "ethnocentrism, authoritarianism, and support for extreme political violence."[7]

I understand this to mean that genuinely positive growth after trauma must involve a sense of agency that moves a survivor beyond defensive "knee-jerk" reactions. Although moving out of victimhood into taking action might feel passionately meaningful and get us back on our feet, without self-awareness, such actions may, in fact, contribute to continuing polarization and even violence. Whereas, actions born of patient self-work and inner listening are more likely to give rise to the emergence of new beliefs and nonreactive kinds of actions. "Genuine growth," the study suggests, "only occurs when cognitive changes are transformed into action."[8]

─────── *Israel and the Trauma Factor* ───────

Many victims of physical abuse and ethnic violence go on to harbor hatred of the other and even go on to commit violent behaviors themselves.[9] In this sense, Rami and Mazen may be seen as cultural anomalies.

What determines the choices we make? How does a person choose to resist vengeance, to turn aside from repetitive cycles of violence? Given the natural byproducts of trauma— emotional numbness, hyperarousal, and self-defensiveness, which make awareness of other people's suffering almost impossible—it is a marvel that people actually manage to jump off the trauma train.

As researcher Erwin Staub tells us, "Unhealed wounds make it more difficult to take the other's perspective, to consider the other's needs, and to feel empathy for the other. Perceiving a threat, people may engage in what they believe is self-defense—but their 'defensive violence' may be unnecessary or more forceful than necessary."[10]

This is all too true in Israel, where the objective situation of threat from hostile neighbors is complicated and exacerbated by trauma's residue. Feelings of being under siege and vulnerable to attack at all times—whether on the streets of Sderot, at the checkpoints going into Jerusalem, or in the back alleys of Hebron—all too often lead, says Staub, to "defensive violence" and reactions that are "more forceful than necessary." These actions, in turn, feed the cycle of violence and the self-fulfilling prophecy that "all *goyim* hate us and want us dead," a Jewish belief I have heard so often.

I found in my interviews that the trauma factor—that is, the disproportionality of action and reaction—often complicates Israel's military policies in the West Bank. As Yehuda, a veteran officer in the IDF told me, "You have a ten-year-old with a stone and soldiers with combat gear and Uzis— sometimes even inside a tank—who feel threatened. It doesn't make sense."

Notwithstanding this kind of reactivity, Israel's instinct to defend itself is healthy and cannot be judged. Nor can young Israelis be blamed who are determined to be brave and live out their country's highest ideal of bringing their people *mai-Shoah l'tekumah*, from destruction to renewal. But like many Jews around the world for whom the traumatic past is still alive, Israeli soldiers carry the "image deposits" of their elders within themselves, the internalized pictures of Jewish history that scream out against helplessness and demand action. It is arguable whether this kind of action will halt or perpetuate the cycle of violence.

In the Jewish state, the trauma train is still rumbling through. The natural reactivity that goes hand in glove with trauma's aftermath—maintaining a hypermuscular stance, feeling weak even when fully armed, isolated even when backed by the world's superpowers—is understandable. Nevertheless, it is important to recognize what it is costing the Jewish people, and to look ahead to what will bring true security.

Leading the way are people like Rami, Tamara, Avner, and Robi, moral leaders who have come through the eye of the needle of their own pain and hold a view of a possible future. They remind us that the work may take generations, but that we are all part of a living chain of people who have never stopped dreaming and working for a better world. As Rabbi

Tarfon, who lived roughly a thousand years ago, said: "You are not expected to complete the task of repairing the world. But neither are you allowed to put it down."[11]

─────────── *Jewish Global Citizens* ───────────

"We Jews need to take care of Jews. Let the *Goyim* take care of themselves," was the approach I heard repeatedly in my parents' home. Sol and Kate were, in fact, magnanimous givers. My father, a traveling salesman and not wealthy by any means, took pride in tithing between ten and twenty per cent of his annual earnings, bringing upon himself more than one IRS audit.

My parents' answer to their own trauma history was to establish Jewish institutions in our Midwest hometown—an Orthodox synagogue, a Hebrew day school, and a Jewish high school for girls. In addition, they were ardent supporters of the State of Israel, bought Israel bonds and contributed regularly to free loan funds, orphanages, and care centers.

While many in the Jewish community share my parents' views, I have also met many Jews who would identify with Sandi, a woman in her early forties, who described herself as "a global citizen." Sandi's family had emigrated to Mexico from Lithuania in the 1930s, just three years before the Nazi invasion there and the Kaunas pogrom, in which many of her relatives were killed.

Some fifty years later, when Sandi was ten, they relocated in the United States. Sandi became involved in Jewish youth groups and was inspired by the Jewish concept of *tikkun olam*, repair of the world. During college she learned about the

American Jewish World Service (AJWS), a nonprofit organization that is dedicated to ending poverty, assisting in the aftermath of natural and human-made disasters, and promoting human rights in the developing world.

In 1995, Sandi joined a small AJWS delegation of interns who traveled to Honduras to build a potable water system there. "That was the beginning," Sandi told me. "Since then, I've been all over Latin America and the Caribbean with AJWS: in Guatemala, working with Mayan farmers fighting for their land rights; in Haiti, rebuilding after the earthquake. Now that I'm a mom, I fundraise for their programs. I'm devoted."

"My family's history left me a burden, a heartache. But I turned that into a task," Sandi told me. I asked her to tell me what she meant.

"My family made it out, and I'm alive because of it. As they say, 'There but for fortune.' But I have a responsibility as a Jew to do whatever I can do to spare others. It doesn't matter where in the world that happens."

Similarly, Linda, a counseling psychologist by training, chose to work with Native American communities to restore their native culture and language. When I asked how she got involved, she told me that many years earlier, she had joined a volunteer group on the Pine Ridge Reservation, and had been drawn to return. "I was struck by the incredible poverty there, but also by the spiritual richness. People were so strong; they lived their spiritualty."

Linda's father and his parents had escaped Berlin for Shanghai in 1939. (China was then the only country in the world that did not require a visa.) Her mother, aunt, and their parents fled their small village in Austria right after the

Anschluss. While living briefly in Vienna, they were able to purchase visas to the Dominican Republic. Even though Linda's maternal great-grandparents provided the money for the visas, they and other family members refused to leave their homes in Czechoslovakia, believing steadfastly that the world would never allow the Nazis to invade their country. In the end, about 100 of Linda's relatives were trapped in Europe and sent to their deaths.

"As a child of Holocaust survivors I feel a certain camaraderie with Native Americans. Their culture and traditions go back untold generations just as ours do. And both of our peoples have known genocide, displacement, and brutal discrimination. Obviously, their history is very different than ours, but I feel there are parallels between the Native American journey and my own family's journey.

"The other thing is this," Linda added. "Knowing about the miraculous reclamation of Hebrew as our national language inspires me to help the Native Americans reclaim theirs. Even though I don't speak fluent Hebrew, I do know the prayers. And I understand the profound connection between language and identity and how devastating it is to have one's language taken away. I am very committed to this work."

In my own work as rabbi, I have met many young Jews like Sandi and Linda whose Jewish identity is bound up, not with religious ritual practices, but with Jewish ethical imperatives. In Israel, I have been moved by the generous work of groups like Tevel b'Tzedek and IsraAID that deploy Israeli citizens around the world to do disaster relief. And in the United States, the work of T'ruah: The Rabbinic Call for Human Rights is proliferating, with global projects as diverse as trafficking, food justice, Bedouin rights, and African asylum seekers in Israel.

Bend the Arc, another American organization, brings together young Jews from around the country to advocate and organize for social justice and equality. I was struck by how this group articulates a new generation's understanding of its ancestral heritage: "American Jews have been part of the nation's biggest struggles for justice, inspired by our ethical tradition and motivated by the stories of our ancestors both ancient and recent. Sometimes we stood alone, and sometimes we marched alongside fearless fellow travelers, working together to shape the course of history. Today, a new generation is reconnecting with and reclaiming that legacy."

Freeing the Light

At the heart of Judaism lies a story that points to the mysterious drive that motivates people like Linda and Sandi, Rami and Mazen, and so many others in this book. It is a tale that is told in Hebrew day schools and Jewish summer camps; it is studied in yeshivas and schools of Kabbalah worldwide to this day. The story is the origin of the mandate of *tikkun olam*, repair of the world, from which so many Jews derive meaning and life purpose. Yet its images are not exclusively Jewish. They hold meaning for anyone.

In the beginning of time, God was everywhere. But God was lonely, and wanted to be known. So God decided to bring the world into being. To make room for creation, God drew in a first breath to make an empty space in which the world might come into being.

Into this empty space, God emanated a brilliant white light. And vessels came into being in which this divine light could be held and contained.

The light flowed continuously like a luminous river, filling every space it could find. The vessels filled up, but then they began to quake. They could barely contain the voluminous stream of dazzling light. Rumbling fiercely, the vessels flew apart, shattering into millions of pieces, sending sparks of the white light like seeds and stars far and wide.

Each spark came to be encased in one of the millions of broken shards, which buried its sparkling light deep within. To this day, we are still finding and uncovering the hard casings around the sparks of the world, freeing their light so that they can shine again.

Our world has been broken from the beginning, the creation myth tells us. Its primal flaw—an inability to contain the numinous light of creation—necessitates our work. *Tikkun olam* names our task: to find and uncover the light inherent in the shards of this world, no matter where it is hidden.

Jews are the proud heirs of thousands of years of tradition. It is a tradition that urges us to take responsibility for the world, to identify with suffering wherever we find it, to see ourselves as copartners in creation, to uncover the light of possibility and hope wherever we can.

This work never ends, but as so many people have taught me along my journey, our wounds can yield new wisdom, release hidden sparks of light, and open up unexpected paths to the future. I have seen it with my own eyes.

ENDNOTES

PART I

Introduction: Shedding New Light on a Dark History

[1] Israeli traumatologist Dan Bar-On wrote: "'Untold stories' often pass more powerfully from generation to generation than stories that can be recounted" (1995, 20). For more about the necessity of articulating one's memories, see also Van der Kolk and Van der Hart (1995, 158–182).

[2] Laub (1995, 63). Dori Laub was a professor of psychiatry and co-founder of the Fortunoff Video Archive for Holocaust Testimonies at Yale University.

[3] Moral injury is the damage done to a person's conscience or moral compass when that person has either perpetrated or witnessed acts that transgress their own moral/ethical value system. "Moral injury" and "moral injury in the context of war" are now formal categories in the care of United States Veterans. See https://www.ptsd.va.gov/professional/co-occurring/moral_injury_at_war.asp

[4] Kellermann (2013, 33–39)

Chapter One: The Price of Silence

[1] A Yiddish term for rabbinical student or apprentice.

[2] In 1980, after strong lobbying on the part of Vietnam veterans and prominent psychiatrists such as Robert J. Lifton and Leonard Neff, the American Psychiatric Association added PTSD to the third edition of its Diagnostic and Statistical Manual of Mental Disorders (DSM-III) classification scheme. The significant change ushered in by the PTSD diagnosis was that an outside event rather than an inherent individual weakness was the agent of cause for PTSD symptoms. Today, the DSM-V includes, among other criteria for the diagnosis, a catastrophic stressor, which remained a dominating psychological experience for decades and even a lifetime due to intrusive recollections, retaining the power to evoke panic, dread, grief, or despair. Other symptoms named are hyperarousal and reactivity and behavioral strategies such as avoidance and social isolation.

[3] See, e.g., the research of Israeli researcher, Natan P. F. Kellermann (ND). Transmission of Holocaust Trauma, *Yad Vashem,* Jerusalem. https://yadvashem.org/yv/en/education/languages/dutch/pdf/kellermann.pdf

[4] Volkan (2006, 159–160)

[5] Volkan (2015)

[6] The many models of intergenerational trauma transmission are taken up in Natan P. F. Kellermann's essay, "Transmissions of Holocaust Trauma," ND, *Yad Vashem Publications*, Jerusalem, Israel. https://yadvashem.org/yv/en/education/languages/dutch/pdf/kellermann.pdf

[7] The term "posthumous victory for Hitler" was coined by rabbi and philosopher, Emil Fackenheim. Fackenheim, a Holocaust survivor himself, asserted that a "614th Commandment" was necessary after the Nazis' destruction: "Thou shalt not hand Hitler posthumous victories." As such, he was proposing that Jews have a moral obligation to continue their faith and practices, and thus frustrate Hitler's goal of eliminating Judaism from the face of the earth. See Fackenheim (1978).

Chapter Two: Trauma, Mind, and Body: The Paradox of Survival

[1] Langer (1991, 174–175)

[2] Lifton (1995, 137)

[3] Neurohormones like cortisol, adrenaline, epinephrine, and norepinephrine as well as oxytocin are endogenous (internally generated) opioids. These stress hormones help mobilize the required energy to deal with extreme stress. For more on this fascinating topic, see Van der Kolk (1994, 253–265).

[4] A "trauma-informed" approach means (1) being aware of the impact of trauma on individuals and groups, as well as understanding pathways to recovery; (2) recognizing the signs and symptoms of trauma; (3) integrating knowledge about trauma into one's policies and practices; and (4) taking all measures to not retraumatize the survivor. Rather than any one technique, a trauma-informed approach employs principles of building safety, trust, and mutual support.

[5] See *The National Intimate Partner and Sexual Violence Survey: 2010 Summary Report,* National Center for Injury Prevention and Control, Centers for Disease Control and Prevention. https://www.cdc.gov/violenceprevention/pdf/nisvs_report2010-a.pdf

[6] Dodge, Bates, and Pettit (1990); Staub and Vollhardt (2008)

[7] Blumberg (1977, 204–215)

[8] See, for example, Natan P. F. Kellermann (2013), in which the nightmare of a trauma survivor's descendent exhibited similar forms of suffering experienced in the concentration camp by his forebear.

[9] Dias and Ressler (January, 2014). The study performed by Dias and Ressler is more secure than others in that acetophenone is a chemical that binds to a particular receptor in the nose that is encoded by a single gene. This is called the "M71 glomeruli," structures where acetophenone-sensitive neurons in the nose connect with neurons in the olfactory bulb.

[10] Geddes (December 1, 2013). "Fear of a smell can be passed down several generations." *New Scientist.* Retrieved from: https://www.

newscientist.com/article/dn24677-fear-of-a-smell-can-be-passed-down-several-generations/

[11] Yehuda et al. (August 2014, 872–880). In a personal note to the author, Dr. Yehuda added: "We found a change in the same region of a stress related gene in parents and their own children. That does not mean that the effect was transmitted. It does not mean the effect was not transmitted. It means that offspring are affected by the effects of trauma exposure in the parent."

[12] Yehuda et al. (2015)

[13] Yehuda (2015). Dr. Yehuda found that children of Holocaust survivors have altered stress-response systems and differences in methylation on the gene that regulates the number of stress-hormone receptors. In a similar study, trauma research in Israel showed that Jewish patients' symptoms are "immeasurably intensified if their parents were Holocaust survivors or if one or more of their parents took part in one of Israel's many wars and suffered from combat PTSD" (Maoz and Arbit, 2014, 136–137). Another Israeli researcher, Dr. Miri Scharf, showed that susceptibility to PTSD and "secondary traumatization was more apparent" in young Israeli men who had come from families that had survived the Holocaust (2007, 617–618).

[14] Hurley (2013)

[15] Danieli emphasizes the heterogeneity of adaptations on the part of Holocaust survivors. She delineates four basic adaptational styles among Jewish survivor families. These include numb families, victim families, fighter families, and families who have made it. See Danieli (1985, 2006).

[16] In a moving autobiographical essay summing up her life philosophy, Danieli states that "awareness of transmitted intergenerational [trauma] processes will inhibit transmission of pathology to succeeding generations" (2006, 37).

Chapter Three: The Importance of Being Witnessed

[1] Van der Kolk (2014, 203)

² Mindfulness techniques are used widely in the treatment of PTSD. For more on mindfulness and mindfulness practices, see Kabat-Zinn (2018); Van der Kolk (2014); Siegel (2011).

³ Laub (1995, 61–75). The story (T152) is one of the many interviews that belong to the Fortunoff Video Archive for Holocaust Testimonies at Yale University, retold here with the kind permission of Dr. Laub.

⁴ Fortunoff (T152)

⁵ *Ibid.*

⁶ Felman (1995, 48)

⁷ Plesch (2017)

⁸ The Jews should not be considered extraordinary, argued Viscount Cranborne, member of Winston Churchill's cabinet and Leader of the House of Lords. The British Empire was already too full of refugees to take in the Jews, he claimed. In the United States, Herbert Pell, President Franklin D. Roosevelt's envoy to the United Nations War Crimes Commission (UNWCC), struggled to convince leaders in both the State Department and UNWCC to prosecute Nazi crimes against humanity, meeting with "delaying techniques and the absence of clear instructions from either the State Department or the President." Only after the world had witnessed the truth of Nazi barbarism in the highly publicized photographs of the concentration camp liberation, was Pell able to push through the Nuremberg Trials in 1945. See Cox (2014, 77–110).

⁹ Laub (1995, 68). Laub's italics.

¹⁰ Felman (1995, 53). Felman's italics.

¹¹ As quoted by D. Laub (1995, 75, 2n).

Chapter Four: Awakenings

¹ The Parents Circle-Families Forum (PCFF) was founded by Yitzchok Frankenthal in 1994, the year his son Arik was kidnapped and killed by Hamas. Today it consists of over 600 Israeli and Palestinian families who painstakingly cross the border to support one

another and educate the public about the possibility for coexistence, peace, and the need for dialogue to bring about a just resolution to the Israeli-Palestinian conflict. For more information about the Parents Circle-Family Forum, see http://www.theparentscircle.com

[2] Lifton (1998, 12)

[3] Although many Bedouin citizens have served in the IDF, exemptions are extended to all non-Druze Arabs, Orthodox women, and some male Talmudic students. As with other national armies, other exemptions exist, determined upon religious, physical, and psychological grounds.

[4] Moral injury, a term coined by clinical psychiatrist Jonathan Shay in 2009, is a betrayal of one's internal sense of what is right. It has been defined as "perpetrating, failing to prevent, bearing witness to, or learning about acts that transgress deeply held moral beliefs and expectations" (Litz et al., 2009). The term is used widely in mental health literature about military servicemen and women who have witnessed or perpetrated acts in combat that transgress deeply held moral beliefs. For more information on moral injury in the context of war, see Maguen and Litz (2012): Moral Injury in Veterans of War, *PTSD Research Quarterly* 23, 1.

[5] Operation Cast Lead was launched by Israel in December 2008 to stop rocket fire from Gaza into Israel and weapon smuggling into the Gaza Strip. The incursion lasted twenty-two days, in which time, Gazan schools, businesses, and infrastructure were destroyed. Approximately 1,400 Palestinians were killed, most of them civilians. The Israeli death toll was approximately seventy-five. See https://www.btselem.org/statistics/fatalities/after-cast-lead/by-date-of-event

[6] Israel's Prime Minister Benjamin Netanyahu and other right-wing Knesset members have sought to ban Breaking the Silence and cut off its funding. See Harkov, L. (October 17, 2017). For example, "Netanyahu has refused meetings with European foreign ministers who have met with members of Breaking the Silence." See http://www.jpost.com/Israel-News/Politics-And-Diplomacy/Netanyahu-sets-policy-We-wont-meet-diplomats-who-meet-with-Breaking-the-Silence-488966

7   Tzipi Hotovely, Israel's Deputy Foreign Minister, who called the veteran's group "an enemy of Israel," was seconded by Prime Minister Netanyahu. See "Deputy Foreign Minister Labels Breaking the Silence 'An Enemy' of Israel" *Haaretz* (April 26, 2017).

Chapter Five: The Terrible Gift

1   Shoshan (1989, 198)

PART II

Introduction: The Principles of Jewish Cultural Healing

1   This translation is based on an etymological study of the verse's words (Ex. 34: 6–7). The four-letter name of God might be understood as the mind of the universe, the totality of consciousness that exists through all time and space. The verb for remembers *(pokeyd)* also means: visit, counts, or observes. Likewise, the Hebrew word *avon*, usually translated as sins, can denote sorrow and trouble, or wounding, as much as it does wickedness.

2   Abadian and Miller (2008)

3   Erikson (1995, 183)

4   *Ibid.*, 185.

5   The tendency in trauma survivors to become altruistic has been termed Altruism Born of Suffering (ABS), a relatively new category of post-traumatic research. See Staub and Vollhardt (2008).

6   Frankl (1959, 172)

7   *Ibid.*, 127.

8   Like all ethnic stereotypes, Reuven's portrayal of gypsies under the influence of alcohol is unfair and surely does not encompass the Roma people in its complex entirety.

Principle One: Facing the Loss

[1] From 2004 to 2014 alone, rocket attacks killed twenty-seven Israeli civilians, five foreign nationals, five IDF soldiers, and at least eleven Palestinians (B'Tselem, July 24, 2014). By comparison, there were 1,462 Palestinian civilian fatalities (United Nations Human Rights Commission, 2014). Israel's Ministry of Foreign Affairs reported roughly half that number (761). Operation Autumn Clouds (226), Operation Hot Winter (2008).

[2] Ginter, D. (2007). "דכ הריקפה הנידמה תא יעגפנ הדרחה". Natal.org.il. Retrieved 2012-06-07.

[3] While Hamas lobbed thousands of homemade projectiles into Sderot, Israel penetrated Gaza from the air. In the cycle of violence, rocket attacks alternated with Israeli military actions. The Israeli human rights organization B'Tselem reported from the outbreak of the Second Intifada (September 2000 through March 2013) that 8,749 rockets and 5,047 mortar shells were fired on Israel. During this same period, Israel conducted military incursions into the Gaza Strip, each one incurring civilian casualties. Among them were: Operation Rainbow (spring 2004), Operation Days of Penitence (fall 2004), Operation Summer Rains (summer 2006), Operation Autumn Clouds (fall 2006), Operation Hot Winter (2008), the Gaza War (2008–09), and Operation Pillar of Defense (2012).

Principle Two: Harnessing the Power of Pain

[1] Van der Kolk (2014, 96)

[2] For more on the topic of interoception, see Van der Kolk (2014, 95–96 and 413n).

[3] Coates (2014, June)

[4] Coates (2014, June)

[5] The "First Lebanon War," as it is called in Israel, began on June 6, 1982 and lasted a full three years. In this war, many thousands were lost and maimed, the terrorist organization known as Hezbollah was born, and hope for a peace treaty with Israel's neighbors was substantially reduced.

⁶ Van der Kolk (1989, 390)

Principle Three: Finding New Community

¹ Levine (1997, 14)

² Second- and third-generation Holocaust survivor support groups are prolific. Holocaust survivor meetups, educational and counseling services, genealogical and legal assistance, and other forms of support are available in many cities around the world that have a Jewish community. See https://nextgenerationsgroup.wordpress.com/resources/

³ Medding (2007, 57)

⁴ From 1948 to the late 1970s, roughly 900,000 Jews were expelled or fled voluntarily from Muslim countries. See Stillman (2003).

⁵ Egypt is another country where Jewish culture had flourished for centuries. In 1948, with a Jewish population of roughly 75,000, bombings of Jewish neighborhoods and riots began, killing and wounding hundreds of Jews. Following the War of Independence, 20,000 Jews left the country, with thousands more exiting over the next two decades. Today there are only a handful of Jews remaining in Egypt.

⁶ Founded in 2001, JIMENA: Jews Indigenous to the Middle East and North Africa is a nonprofit organization dedicated to the preservation of Mizrahi and Sephardi culture and history. JIMENA advocates for the nearly one million Jews indigenous to the Middle East and North Africa displaced from their countries of origin in the twentieth century. The organization addresses the existing gaps in the historical narrative of the Middle East and North Africa by sharing Mizrahi and Sephardi stories of oppression, plight, and displacement.

⁷ Since carrying out my interviews for this book, I have learned of another group of former soldiers, known as Combatants for Peace. Founded in 2006 by a group of Israeli veterans and Palestinian ex-resistance fighters, Combatants for Peace members work together to press for nonviolent solutions in the region and the end of the Israeli occupation of Palestinian territories. See cfpeae.org/

Principle Four: Resisting the Call to Fear, Blame, and Dehumanize

[1] The Second Intifada, also called the Al Aksa Intifada, was the second Palestinian uprising against Israel (2000–2005). Both Israelis and Palestinians suffered civilian and combatant casualties: An estimated 3,000 Palestinians died by gunfire and air-targeted killings, and Israel's reactions to Palestinian demonstrations. An estimated 1,000 Israelis were killed by suicide bombings and gunfire; sixty-four foreigners were also killed in the uprising.

[2] A 2010 survey of Jewish high school students found that 49.5% of Israeli Jewish high school students believe that Israeli Arabs should not be entitled to the same rights as Jews in Israel; 56% believe Arabs should not be eligible to the Knesset, the Israeli parliament. The March 2010 Tel Aviv University poll took a sampling of 536 Jewish and Arab respondents between the ages of fifteen and eighteen. Of religious Jewish students, 82% opposed equal rights for Arabs while 39% of secular Jewish students polled agreed. See https://www.haaretz.com/poll-half-of-israeli-high-schoolers-oppose-equal-rights-for-arabs-1.264564 and https://www.ynetnews.com/articles/0,7340,L-3861161,00.html

[3] The Green Line is the pre-1967 border, a line of demarcation made in the 1949 Armistice Agreements between Israel and its neighbors (Egypt, Jordan, Lebanon, and Syria) after the 1948 Arab-Israeli War. It is reportedly named for the green marker used by Israeli and Jordanian officials as they negotiated the armistice and delineated boundaries.

[4] Official Israeli statistics demonstrate the value of the fence in lives saved. In 2002, the year before construction started, 457 Israelis fell to terror; in 2009, only eight Israelis were killed. For more, see Bard (2017) West Bank security fence: Background and overview, *Jewish Virtual Library*. Retrieved from http://www.jewishvirtuallibrary.org/background-and-overview-of-israel-s-security-fence

[5] Israel has occupied the West Bank since 1967, meaning that four out of five West Bank Palestinians have never experienced life free

from Israeli military rule. Israel's occupation is an ever-changing system of rules in which Israeli military and intelligence control roughly 2.6 million Arabs. There is one justice system for Palestinians and another for Israelis. Likewise, each population uses a separate system of roads, and has separate rules for water usage. (Israel and Israeli settlements take 80% of the West Bank's mountain aquifer, leaving 20% for the Palestinian occupants.) Checkpoints are another feature of the occupation. The Israel Defense Forces (IDF) operates numbers of fixed and movable barriers (ranging in the hundreds) throughout the West Bank with the stated purpose of enhancing Israel's security and impeding those who wish to do harm from crossing into Israel. Staffed by Israel Military Police and Border Police, the checkpoints slow and at times immobilize Palestinian movement, creating daily indignities. Israel Prime Minister Benjamin Netanyahu and his constituents call the occupied West Bank region by the biblical name of Judea and Sumeria, believing that God awarded the Jewish people *Eretz Yisroel Shleymah*, the entirety of the Land of Israel. He has called the occupation of the West Bank, the "so-called Occupation."

[6] Qalandia (Kalandia) is the main checkpoint between the northern West Bank and Jerusalem. Israel requires Palestinians to have permits to pass through the checkpoint to East Jerusalem and Israel for their work, medical care, education, or religious reasons; however, internationals are supposed to be able to pass freely in and out of the Occupied Palestinian Territories. Most of the people who use the Qalandia checkpoint are residents of East Jerusalem separated from the city by Israel's security fence.

[7] Klein (2008, 210)

[8] For more information on teen trips to Poland, see the Israeli Ministry of Education's online page describing the trip to Poland program, curricula, and subsidies.

[9] See Chapter Four of Mishna Avot in the Babylonian Talmud, also called the Ethics of the Fathers.

[10] The phrase literally means: "The one who turns an enemy into a lover." It is drawn from a teaching in *Avot de Rabbi Natan* (Jerusalem Talmud)

that asks: "Who is a hero of heroes? The sages answered: Not one who defeats his enemy, but one who turns an enemy into a friend." The two words, *Oyev* (enemy) and *Ohev* (lover, friend), are just one letter apart.

[11] The origin of this famous threat was Sheikh Hassan al-Banna, founder of the Muslim Brotherhood, who told *New York Times* correspondent Dana Adams Schmidt in Cairo on August 1, 1948: "If the Jewish state becomes a fact, and this is realized by the Arab peoples, they will drive the Jews who live in their midst into the sea." Schmidt added that the sheikh was referring to the quarter-million Jews still living in Arab countries at the time, that he had said this "facetiously, and that 'of course, if the United States send ships to pick them up, that would be all right.'" But the sheikh's words reverberated for the Jews. Ever since, the comment has been repeated by Israeli statesmen and Jews worldwide. As David Ben-Gurion phrased it when presenting his new government to the Knesset on November 2, 1955: " ... and they plan, as many of them say openly, to throw us all into the sea; in simpler words, to exterminate the Jews of the Land of Israel." To read more, see: https://www.haaretz.com/israel-news/word-for-word-who-s-throwing-who-into-the-sea-1.449269)

[12] The Forgiveness Project is dedicated to awareness, education, and transformation through the use of real stories of victims and perpetrators to explore concepts of forgiveness and to encourage people to consider alternatives to resentment, retaliation, and revenge. For more information about the Forgiveness Project, see http://theforgiveness-project.com

[13] Gilad Shalit is a former MIA soldier of the IDF who was captured by Hamas militants on June 25, 2006 in a cross-border raid near the Israeli border. Hamas held Shalit captive for over five years, until his release on October 18, 2011, as part of a prisoner exchange deal.

Principle Five: Disidentifying from Victimhood

[1] I have chosen to spell the term anti-Semitism as such, while recognizing that the use of the hyphen and upper case in the spelling

of anti-Semitism has been called into question by scholars such as Yehuda Bauer, who claim that it legitimizes a false and nonscientific category of Semitism.

[2] The term *anti-Semitism* was first popularized in the 1870s by a German journalist named Wilhelm Marr, who warned of the dangerous infiltration of the "Jewish spirit." Marr asserted that Germany was suffering from an existential racial struggle, and that the Jews were winning due to the Emancipation, which had allowed them to make gains in industry and finance. This struggle, Marr proclaimed, would only be resolved by the victory of one and the annihilation of the other. (At the time, Jews comprised less than 1% of the German population.) Marr was obviously articulating a popular fear, which conflated Jews with liberal, cosmopolitan trends such as equal civil rights, free trade, and pacifism. Notably, at the end of his life, Marr, who had married three Jewish women in succession, recanted his anti-Semitism and apologized for his stigmatization of Jews. According to Moshe Zimmerman (1986, 103 and 135), Marr "openly requested the Jews' pardon for having erred in isolating the problem" and targeting the Jews.

[3] I am grateful to Petsonk and Remsen (1988, 17–30) for their astute elucidation of Jews in the Christian Empire.

[4] Luther's edicts published in 1543 (1971, 268–271), advocated seven curative actions: "To set fire to [Jewish] synagogues and schools and bury whatever will not burn; destroy Jewish homes; take away all prayer books and Talmudic writings; offer no protection to Jews on the highways; prohibit rabbis from teaching; prohibit the Jewish practice of moneylending; and take away all savings for safekeeping until there is an authentic conversion. William Shirer noted in *The Rise and Fall of the Third Reich*, "Luther's advice was literally followed four centuries later by Hitler, Goering and Himmler" (1959/1990, 236). Lutheran theologians themselves recognize the continuity between Protestant anti-Judaism and the racially oriented anti-Semitism that influenced Nazism and exists today. Johannes Wallmann (1987, 72) writes that this connection "is at present widespread in the literature; since the

Second World War, it has understandably become the prevailing opinion." Other historians who posit the same connection are Johnson (1987, 242); Berenbaum (1993/2000, 8–9); and Moen (2012).

[5] The number of anti-Semitic incidents in the United Kingdom rose to record levels (more than 33%) in 2016, according to data released by the Community Security Trust. See https://www.theguardian.com/world/2017/feb/02/reports-of-antisemitic-incidents-increase-to-record-levels-in-uk

On the European continent, from January to June 2017, there was a 30% increase in anti-Semitic incidents, as compared with the same period in 2016. See https://european-forum-on-antisemitism.org/reports and https://www.theguardian.com/world/2017/feb/02/reports-of-antisemitic-incidents-increase-to-record-levels-in-uk

[6] Anti-Semitic attacks in the United States rose by 33% in 2016 and 86% in the first quarter of 2017 alone, according to a survey carried out by the Anti-Defamation League.

[7] Goldberg, J.J. (October 28, 2018). "Pittsburgh Synagogue Murder Spree Latest in 4 Decades of Organized Anti-Semitic Attacks." *The Forward.*

[8] Since the anti-Semitic events of 2015, roughly 6,000 to 7,000 French Jews have emigrated to Israel and other countries per year. According to Eliette Abécassis, in *The Temptation to Leave*, many French Jews are convinced that they can remain Jewish in their country, and that racially inspired terrorist attacks in France are a concern not only to Jews but to the general public. See Semotiuk, A. J. (February 12, 2018). Jews in France ponder whether to stay or leave. *Forbes.*

[9] The reported rise in Jewish immigration to Israel was largely from Ukraine and Russia, not Western Europe. See Zonszein (May 3, 2015), *The Guardian.*

[10] Following the Paris supermarket tragedy, and again after the Copenhagen synagogue attack, Prime Minister Benjamin Netanyahu declared: "I say to the Jews of Europe—Israel is your home." See: Tova Lazaroff (January 10, 2015), *Jerusalem Post.*

[11] No author listed (January 11, 2015). "European Jewish Group Slams Netanyahu's Call for French Jews to Immigrate to Israel." *Haaretz.*

[12] See Ravid (February 15, 2015). "Danish Chief Rabbi Responds to Netanyahu: Terror is Not a Reason to Move to Israel." *Haaretz.*

[13] Thanks to Rabbi Brant Rosen for his clarity about these distinctions. See "European Anti-Semitism: Is it happening again?" in *On Anti-Semitism: Solidarity and the Struggle for Justice* (2017). Jewish Voice for Peace, Haymarket Books: Chicago, IL.

[14] For example, a psychological survey in 2017 run by psychologists Patrick Forscher and Nur Kteily demonstrated the profile of white supremacist hate groups in America. See Resnik (August 15, 2017). *Vox.* Retrieved from: https://www.vox.com/science-and-health/2017/8/15/16144070/psychology-alt-right

[15] Frankl (2006, 69)

Principle Six: Redefining Jewish Chosenness

[1] Chosenness in some form is actually a cornerstone of all three of the Abrahamic traditions. See Reuven Firestone's *Who are the Real Chosen People? The Meaning of Chosenness in Judaism, Christianity, and Islam,* Woodstock, (2008).

[2] Erikson (1966, 606) termed the concept encapsulating the tendency of a group to self-define as its own species as "pseudo-speciation." According to Erikson, when the core of any collective identity centers around its pseudo-speciation, oppression is bound to play a part in that people's history.

[3] The book of Genesis is full of irony and intrigue surrounding the struggle between brothers for the father's prophetic blessing. More often than not, a tricksterish element injects itself and turns the family's fate on its head in such a way as to overturn the firstborn son's benefits so that a deeper law can have its way.

[4] This is the fast of the firstborn or *Ta'anit Bechorot.* This day is a traditional fast day for all Jewish firstborn males, though study can and usually does take the place of fasting.

[5] It is possible that such ceremonies are vestiges of ancient polytheistic rites, when firstborn children were seen as precious and sacrificed to the gods. The ritual has persisted in Orthodox Judaism.

[6] The Holy Rabbi Moses Sofer (1762–1839) was the chief rabbi of Pressburg (also called Bratislava) in Austro-Hungary, and established the Pressburg yeshiva, the most prominent center of Talmudic training in central Europe. A halachic authority, the Chasam Sofer was known for his uncompromising opposition to the newly burgeoning movement of Reform Judaism as well as to any change in Orthodox praxis.

[7] The deadly attack on the Dawabsheh family was a crime of vengeance following the demolition of two illegal Jewish structures in the settlement of Beit El by Israeli officials less than forty-eight hours earlier. Jewish settlers had failed in their attempts to thwart the bulldozers.

[8] The "Price Tag Gang" *(Tag Machir)* is the name taken by young fundamentalist Israeli settlers who commit acts of random violence on the Palestinian population. Their aim is to exact a price for any action that takes a stand against the settlement enterprise or avenges their campaigns, which include building settler outposts on Palestinian lands or demolishing Palestinian property. For these people, all crimes are excusable to achieve a Jewish upper hand in Judea and Sumeria.

[9] Levy (2015)

[10] The Lau-Lavie story is chronicled in *Balaam's Prophecy: Eyewitness to History, 1939-1989* by Naphtali Lau-Lavie, Amichai's father, whose entire family perished in Europe except for his brother Yisrael, who later became the Chief Rabbi of Israel. Amichai Lau-Lavie is now the founding rabbi of a progressive synagogue community in New York City, Lab/Shul (labshul.org), which is built on the vision and practice of Storahtelling, another of Lau-Lavie's innovative projects, which combines the ancient art of sacred storytelling with contemporary theatre.

[11] The story of *Akedat Yitzchok*, the binding of Isaac (Yitzchok in Hebrew) for sacrifice is found in Genesis 22.

[12] See, e.g., the work of Ervin Staub and Johanna Vollhardt (2008) on the topic of altruism that arises from traumatic experiences. Altruism born of suffering: The roots of caring and helping after victimization and other trauma. *American Journal of Orthopsychiatry*, 78(3), 267–280. doi:10.1037/a0014223.

Principle Seven: Taking Action

[1] Midrash Socher Tov 22:7.

[2] Kellermann (2013, 33)

[3] The term post-traumatic growth (PTG) was coined by psychologists Richard Tedeschi and Lawrence Calhoun at the University of North Carolina at Charlotte in the mid-1990s. PTG is characterized by several growth-after-trauma markers: Appreciation of life, relationships to others, finding new possibilities in life, personal strength, and spiritual changes. See Michaela Haas, (2015). *"Bouncing forward: Transforming bad breaks into breakthroughs,"* Atria/Enliven.

[4] See Tedeschi, Park, and Calhoun, eds. (1998,12f).

[5] Yehuda (2014) retrieved from: http://tablet-mag.com/jewish-arts-and-culture/books/187555/trauma-genes-q-a-rachel-yehuda

[6] These findings were especially associated to those with low self-efficacy. See Hobfoll, et al. (2007, 345–366).

[7] *Ibid.*, 352.

[8] Staub and Vollhardt (2008, 270)

[9] On a collective scale, past victimization appears to be one of the central influences contributing to mass violence. See: Staub and Vollhardt (2008), who quote studies of Mamdani (2002), Rouhana and Bar-Tal (1998), Staub (1998), Staub and Pearlman (2006), and Volkan (1998).

[10] Staub, 2011, 276.

[11] Mishnah Avot 2:21

REFERENCES

Abadian, S. and Miller, T. (Winter/Spring 2008). "Taming the beast: Trauma in Jewish religious and political life." *Journal of Jewish Communal Service* 83 (2/3).

B'Tselem. (July 24, 2014). "Attacks on Israeli civilians by Palestinians."

Bar-On, D. (1995). *Fear and hope: Three generations of the Holocaust.* Cambridge, MA: Harvard University Press.

Bard, M. (2017). "West Bank security fence: Background and overview." *Jewish Virtual Library*.

Berenbaum, M. (1993/2000). *The world must know.* Baltimore, MD: Johns Hopkins University Press and the United States Holocaust Museum.

Blumberg, M. L. (1977). "Treatment of the abused child and the child abuser." *American Journal of Psychotherapy* 31: 204–215.

Coates, T-N. (June, 2014). The case for reparations. *The Atlantic*.

Cox, G. (June, 2014). "Seeking justice for the Holocaust: Herbert C. Pell vs. the U.S. State Department." *Criminal Law Forum* 25 (1–2): 77–110.

Danieli, Y. (1985). "The treatment and prevention of long-term effects and intergenerational transmission of victimization: A lesson from Holocaust survivors and their children." In C. R. Figley (Ed.), *Trauma and its wake, Volume 1: The study and treatment of post-traumatic stress disorder,* 36–41. New York, NY: Brunner/ Mazel.

Danieli, Y. (2006). "It was always there." In C. R. Figley (Ed.), *Mapping trauma and its wake: Autobiographical essays by pioneer trauma scholars,* 33–45. New York, NY: Routledge, Taylor & Francis Group.

Dias, B. G. and Ressler, K. J. (March 5, 2014). "Parental olfactory experience influences behavior and neural structure in subsequent generations." *Nature Neuroscience* 17: 89–96.

Dodge, K. A., Bates, J. E., and Pettit, G. S. (1990). "Mechanisms in the cycle of violence." *Science* magazine 250 (4988): 1678–1683.

Erikson, E. (1966). "Ontogeny of ritualization." In R. M. Lowenstein, L. M. Newman, M. Schur, and A. J. Solnit (Eds.), *Psychoanalysis: A general psychology*, 232–254. New York, NY: International Universities Press.

Erikson, K. (1995). "Notes on trauma and community." In C. Caruth (Ed.), *Trauma: Explorations in memory,* 183–198. Baltimore, MD: Johns Hopkins University Press.

Fackenheim, E. (1978). *The Jewish return into history: Reflections in an age of Auschwitz and a new Jerusalem.* New York, NY: Schocken Books.

Felman, S. (1995). "Education and crisis, or the vicissitudes of teaching." In C. Caruth (Ed.), *Trauma: Explorations in memory*, 13–60. Baltimore, MD: Johns Hopkins University Press.

Firestone, R. (2008). *Who are the real chosen people? The meaning of chosenness in Judaism, Christianity, and Islam.* Woodstock, VT: Skylight Paths.

Frankl, V. E. (1959/2006). *Man's search for meaning.* Boston, MA: Beacon Press.

Geddes, L. (Dec. 1, 2013). "Fear of a smell can be passed down several generations." *New Scientist.*

Gilligan, J. (1996). *Violence: Our deadly epidemic and its causes.* New York, NY: Putnam.

Ginter, Davida (Nov. 26, 2007). "הדרחה יעגפנ תא הנידמה הריקפה רכ." Natal.org.il.

Goldberg, J. J. (Oct. 28, 2018). "Pittsburgh synagogue murder spree latest in 4 decades organized anti-Semitic attacks." *The Forward*.

Haas, M. (2015). *Bouncing forward: Transforming bad breaks into breakthroughs*, New York, NY: Atria/Enliven Books.

Harkov, L. (Oct. 17, 2017). Netanyahu pushes for bill to ban Breaking the Silence, BDS NGOs. *Jerusalem Post*.

Herman, J. L. (1992). *Trauma and recovery: The aftermath of violence—from domestic abuse to political terror*. New York, NY: Basic Books.

Hobfoll, S., Hall, B., Canetti-Nisim, D., Galea, S., Johnson, R., and Palmiari, P. (2007). "Refining the understanding of traumatic growth in the face of terrorism: Moving from meaning cognitions to doing what is meaningful." *Applied Psychology: An International Review*, 56(3): 345–366.

Hurley, D. (June 11, 2013). "Grandma's experiences leave a mark on your genes." *Discover*.

Johnson, P. (1987). *A history of the Jews*. New York, NY: Harper Collins.

Kabat-Zinn, J. (2018). *The healing power of mindfulness: A new way of being*. New York, NY: Hachette Books.

Kellermann, N. P. F. (2013). "Epigenetic transmission of holocaust trauma: Can nightmares be inherited?" *Israel Journal of Psychiatry and Related Sciences*, 50(1): 33–39.

Klein. N. (2008). *The shock doctrine: The rise of disaster capitalism*. New York, NY: Picador.

Langer, L. L. (1991). *Holocaust testimonies: The ruins of memory*. New Haven, CT: Yale University Press.

Lau-Lavie, N. (2015). *Balaam's prophecy: Eyewitness to history, 1939–1989*. New Milford, CT: Toby Press.

Laub, D. (1995). "Truth and testimony: The process and the struggle." In C. Caruth (Ed.), *Trauma: Explorations in memory*, 61–75. Baltimore, MD: Johns Hopkins University Press.

Lazaroff, T. (Jan. 10, 2015). "Netanyahu to French/European Jews after Paris attacks: Israel is your home." *Jerusalem Post*. Retrieved from: http://www.jpost.com/Israel-News/

Netanyahu-to-French-European-Jews-after-Paris-attacks-Israel-is-your-home-387309

Levine, P. (1997). *Waking the tiger: Healing trauma: The innate capacity to transform overwhelming experiences.* Berkeley, CA: North Atlantic Books.

Levy, G. (Aug. 2, 2015). "All Israelis are guilty of setting a Palestinian family on fire." *Haaretz.*

Lifton, R. J. (1995). "An interview with Robert Jay Lifton." In C. Caruth (Ed.), *Trauma: Explorations in memory*, 128–150). Baltimore, MD: Johns Hopkins University Press.

Lifton, R.J. (1998). Foreword. In Danieli, Y. (Ed.), *International handbook of multigenerational legacies of trauma*, 12. New York, NY: Plenum Press.

Litz, B. T., Stein, N., Delaney, E., Lebowitz, L., Nash, W. P., Silva, C., et al. (2009). "Moral injury and moral repair in war veterans: A preliminary model and intervention strategy." *Clinical Psychology Review* 29: 695–706.

Luther, M. (1971). "On Jews and their lies." In *Luther's Works*, Volume 47: *The Christian in Society IV.* Philadelphia, PA: Fortress Press.

Maguen, S. and Litz, B. (2012). Moral injury in veterans of war, *PTSD Research Quarterly* 23(1).

Maoz, G., and Arbit, V. (2014). "Between aggression and compassion: Treating post-trauma within a trauma-stricken space." In G. Gudaite and M. Stein (Eds.), *Confronting cultural trauma: Jungian approaches to understanding and healing*, 131–148. New Orleans, LA: Spring Journal Books.

Medding, P.Y. (2007). *Sephardic Jewry and Mizrahi Jews* 22: 57. New York, NY: Oxford University Press.

Moen, M. (Dec. 17, 2012). "A merciful severity: How Martin Luther influenced Adolf Hitler's persecution of the Jews." *Liberty Baptist Theological Seminary.*

Petsonk, J. and Remsen, J. (1988). *The intermarriage handbook: A guide for Jews & Christians.* New York, NY: William Morrow & Company.

Plesch, D. (2017). *Human rights after Hitler: The lost history of prosecuting axis war crimes*. Washington, D.C.: Georgetown University Press.

Ravid, B. (Feb. 15, 2015). Danish chief rabbi responds to Netanyahu: Terror is not a reason to move to Israel. *Haaretz*.

Resnik, B. (Aug. 15, 2017). *Vox*.

Rosen, Rabbi B. (2017). "European anti-Semitism: Is it happening again?" In *On anti-Semitism: Solidarity and the struggle for justice*. Chicago, IL: Haymarket Books, Jewish Voice for Peace.

Scharf, M. (2007). "Long-term effects of trauma: Psychological functioning of the second and third generation of Holocaust survivors." *Development and Psychopathology*, 19(1): 603–622.

Shirer, W. L. (1959/1990). *The rise and fall of the Third Reich*. New York, NY: Simon & Schuster.

Shoshan, T. (April, 1989). "Mourning and longing from generation to generation." *American Journal of Psychotherapy*, 43(2): 193-207.

Siegel, D. J. (2011). *Mindsight: The new science of personal transformation*. New York, NY: Bantam Books.

Staub, E. (2011). *Overcoming evil: Genocide, violent conflict and terrorism*. New York, NY: Oxford University Press.

Staub, E. and Vollhardt, J. (2008). "Altruism born of suffering: The roots of caring and helping after victimization and other trauma." *American Journal of Orthopsychiatry*, 78(3): 267–280.

Stillman, N. (2003). *The Jews of Arab lands in modern times*. New York, NY: The Jewish Publication Society.

Tedeschi, R. G., Park, C. L., and Calhoun, L.G., eds. (1998). *Posttraumatic growth: Positive transformation in the aftermath of crisis*. Mahwah, NJ: Erlbaum.

United Nations Human Rights Commission on Israel's Incursion into Gaza (Summer, 2014).

Van der Kolk, B. A. (June, 1989). "The compulsion to repeat the trauma: Re-enactment, revictimization, and masochism." *Psychiatric Clinics of North America*, 12(2): 389–411.

Van der Kolk, B. A. (1994). "The body keeps the score: Memory and the evolving psychobiology of post-traumatic stress." *Harvard Review of Psychiatry*, 1(5): 253–265.

Van der Kolk, B. A. and Van der Hart, O. (1995). "The intrusive past: The flexibility of memory and the engraving of trauma." In C. Caruth (Ed.), *Trauma: Explorations in memory*, 158–172. Baltimore, MD: Johns Hopkins University Press.

Van der Kolk, B. A. (2014). *The body keeps the score: Brain, mind, and body in the healing of trauma*. New York, NY: Viking Books.

Volkan, V. D. (2006). *Killing in the name of identity: A study of bloody conflicts*. Charlottesville, VA: Pitchstone Publishing.

Volkan, V. D. (2015). *A Nazi legacy: Depositing, transgenerational transmission, dissociation, and remembering through action*. London, England: Karnac Books.

Wallmann, J. (Spring, 1987). "The reception of Luther's writings on the Jews from the Reformation to the end of the 19th century." *Lutheran Quarterly*, 1(1): 72–97.

Yehuda, R., Daskalakis, N. P., Lehrner, A., Desarnaud, F., Bader, H. N., Makotkine, I., Flory, J. D., Bierer, L.M., and Meaney, M. J. (August, 2014). "Influences of maternal and paternal PTSD on epigenetic regulation of the glucocorticoid receptor gene in Holocaust survivor offspring." *American Journal of Psychiatry*, 171: 872–880.

Yehuda, R. (Dec. 11, 2014). "Do Jews carry trauma in our genes? A conversation with Rachel Yehuda." *Tablet*.

Yehuda, R. (July 31, 2015). "How trauma and resilience cross generations." *On Being with Krista Tippett*.

Zimmerman, M. (1986). *Wilhelm Marr: The patriarch of anti-Semitism*. Oxford, England: Oxford University Press.

Zonszein, M. (May 3, 2015). "Jewish migration to Israel up 40% this year so far." *The Guardian*.

[Author Unavailable]. (Jan. 11, 2015). "European Jewish group slams Netanyahu's call for French Jews to immigrate to Israel." *Haaretz*.

[Author Unavailable]. (April 26, 2017). "Deputy Foreign Minister labels Breaking the Silence 'an enemy' of Israel." *Haaretz*.

ACKNOWLEDGMENTS

The body of work contained in this book has evolved over many years with the support and encouragement of teachers, friends, and guides. I am immensely grateful to all those who helped me bring this book to light.

The idea that an entire group of people could suffer the effects of post-traumatic stress disorder (PTSD) and that their unhealed psychological suffering could shape a culture was first articulated by my teacher and friend Rabbi Irwin Kula in Boulder, Colorado, just days before 9/11. His words sparked an entire journey, one that continues to reveal itself.

Dr. Mary Watkins, my beloved professor and dissertation chairperson, encouraged my thinking and challenged me to dig deeper, think bigger. Professor Dori Laub, the late Holocaust scholar and co-founder of the Fortunoff Video Archive for Holocaust Testimonies at Yale University, was a profound inspiration from the start. He helped me understand the critical importance of bearing witness in the process of trauma healing and gave me firsthand insight into the survivor's testimony that

I share in Chapter Four. Sadly, my conversations with Professor Laub were cut short by his sudden death in June, 2018.

Although I am surely not a scientist, the epigenetic research and insights of Dr. Rachel Yehuda have inspired a deep awe in me. I was honored to have Dr. Yehuda read and comment on several sections of my manuscript. I am also grateful to Dr. Jeffrey Raff, Rabbi Dr. Mel Gottlieb, Laya Seghi, Pastor James Ray, Dr. Jeanine Canty, and Dr. Naomi Rusk for reading and discussing my manuscript as it evolved.

My beloved partner David Friedman has been a godsend all these many years. David's practical, emotional, and spiritual care of me have been my lifelines, as have his sense of humor, foot rubs, and common-sense approach. I thank God every day for his loving friendship.

I have abundant gratitude for my brilliant and highly attuned editor Toni Burbank, without whom this work would never have come to light. Toni believed in this book long before its contours were clear to me. Working with Toni has felt like playing music under the baton of a master conductor— form and beauty magically took shape out of chaos.

It is my ardent hope that *Wounds into Wisdom* will serve to ignite a conversation and stimulate new awareness about the power of our ancestral legacies. To that end, my publishers at Monkfish/Adam Kadmon Books, Paul Cohen and Netanel Miles Yepez, have been profound allies in midwifing this book with deep intelligence and an impeccable work ethic. My thanks to Susan Piperato, Colin Rolfe, and Dory Mayo for their expert editing, typesetting and layout, and proofreading, as well as to Meryl Zegarek, Ginger Price, and Rae Abileah for skillfully and wholeheartedly helping to bring this work to the world at large.

ABOUT THE AUTHOR

Rabbi Tirzah Firestone, Ph.D., is an author, Jungian psycho-therapist, and founding rabbi of Congregation Nevi Kodesh in Boulder, Colorado. Ordained by Rabbi Zalman Schachter-Shalomi in 1992, she is a leader in the international Jewish Renewal Movement known as Aleph: Alliance for Jewish Renewal, and has served on the board of directors and as co-chair of Rabbis for Human Rights, North America (now known as T'ruah: The Rabbinic Call for Human Rights).

Raised in a large Orthodox family in St. Louis, Missouri, the younger sister of the late, groundbreaking radical feminist Shulamith Firestone, author of *The Dialectic of Sex* (William Morrow & Company, 1970), Firestone's spiritual curiosity called her to search beyond the confines of her family's strict Jewish upbringing. Leaving home, she embarked upon a life-changing spiritual odyssey that she chronicled in *With Roots in Heaven: One Woman's Passionate Journey into the Heart of Her Faith* (Dutton Books, 1998). After immersing herself in a wide variety of spiritual practices and worldviews, Firestone returned with fresh vigor to a pluralistic and egalitarian Judaism, continuing in the tradition of Rabbi Schachter-Shalomi. Her studies in the feminine wisdom tradition and Jewish mysticism yielded *The Receiving: Reclaiming Jewish Women's Wisdom* (Harper San Francisco, 2003).

Firestone earned a master's degree in counseling at Beacon College in Boston, Massachusetts in 1982, and a doctorate in depth psychology at Pacifica Graduate Institute in Santa Barbara, California in 2015. Her research on the transformation of collective trauma draws on the fields of neuroscience, psychology, Jewish literature, and mythopoesis. Through interviews, case studies, and autobiographical stories, she demonstrates how trauma residue passes from generation to generation and how it can be transformed.

Now Rabbi Emerita of her congregation, Firestone maintains a private practice in depth psychology and teaches nationally about ancestral healing: how to transform patterns of suffering from our past and bring forth the clarity, wisdom, and blessings of our ancestral lineages. Rabbi Firestone lives in Colorado with her husband David. Together they have three grown children: Brianna, Emily, and Dakota. For more information, visit TirzahFirestone.com.